VADEMECUM

Vademecum

VADEMECUM

77 Minor Terms for Writing Urban Places

edited by
Klaske Havik, Kris Pint, Svava Riesto
and Henriette Steiner

Writing urban places with minor terms

Klaske Havik, Kris Pint, Svava Riesto and Henriette Steiner

As we write these lines – during the early days of the coronavirus outbreak, with the public life and infrastructure of European cities in lockdown – we are confronting a situation where personal, societal and spatial relationships are being fundamentally reconfigured.
We once again come to realise how intricate are the relationships we establish with our built environment, and how much we take our attachments to urban places for granted. The coronavirus crisis also reminds us of other global crises, such as global warming and resource depletion, which sooner or later may strongly affect our living conditions.
Even aside from these global challenges, European cities and the ways people live in them have been changing rapidly in recent years, due to various simultaneous processes such as increasingly market-driven urban development, growing inequality, migration, segregation and surveillance capitalism. In order to act in this unstable urban terrain, spatial professionals such as urban planners, architects, landscape architects, heritage managers and policymakers may need to seek alternatives to conventional codes and models of spatial development. These univocal diagnoses and rigid planning methods, based on precise cost-benefit calculations and hypotheses regarding the predictable effects of architectural interventions, are no longer reliable or feasible, and often fail to

address specific social and spatial circumstances in urban places. This book is based on a strong belief that if we are to foster more socially inclusive and site-specific urban approaches, we need new ways to understand the particularities and complexities of each urban situation. Our aim is to move beyond essentialist or generalising metanarratives that have long dominated urban discourse, and to instead look for multiple, minor narratives that are specific to sites and communities, therefore allowing for a diversity of situated perspectives. A way to do this, we suggest, is to think carefully about the words we use to understand urban places. This *Vademecum* is intended to offer a set of concepts that may be useful to stimulate new approaches in planning, architecture, urban design, policy and other practices of spatial development.
The *Vademecum* has been compiled by an interdisciplinary group of European scholars connected through the European Union's (EU) Cooperation in Science and Technology (COST) Action network Writing Urban Places: New Narratives of the European City. This network focuses particularly on the potential of narrative methods for urban development in medium-sized European cities. The common interest of the group is to understand the urban as a complex and interim expression of culturally and historically situated social, material, spatial and temporal relations between people and their built environment. Our motivation to approach urban questions through narrative lies in the idea that urban cultures and urban narratives are intertwined: stories contain valuable information regarding citizens' socio-spatial practices, perceptions and expectations as much as they affect these forms of urban life. The network comprises scholars from a range of disciplines including literary and cultural theory, architecture, urbanism, sociology, art, digital studies, film and media studies, and we have taken this opportunity to collect a number of terms and theoretical concepts from the members of the network. We believe that concepts that have thus far been relatively unknown in common urbanist discourse may nonetheless prove useful for

the exploration of urban narratives and the writing of new stories.

The phrase *vade mecum* is Latin for 'go with me' (it derives from the Latin verb *vadere*, meaning 'to go'). In English, *vade mecum* has been used (since at least 1629) as a name for manuals or guidebooks that are sufficiently compact to be carried in a deep pocket. Today, the framework of the EU COST Actions is summarised in a companion document entitled *Vademecum*. Thus, the term 'vademecum' has migrated between different domains and changed its meanings along the way. This book is meant to be a positive projection and exploration of that term's usefulness in numerous contexts since the 17th century. We chose this term as a parameter for how we understand concepts as such: concepts are not stable, and processes of naming can themselves change and challenge the notions, understandings and even normative frameworks we carry with us.

Minor concepts

In this *Vademecum* we present a set of concepts that help us to explore new ways of thinking about and experiencing urban places, by introducing a diversity of concepts that might reveal blind spots in urban discourse or bring insights from one discipline to another. Different theoretical concepts are used in different discursive domains that deal with the urban landscape: they help to make sense of what happens in the city, but they also imply a specific outlook on the city. While they are useful tools, concepts inevitably create their own limited horizons. As the well-known phrase from psychologist Abraham Maslow's *The psychology of science* indicates – 'for a hammer, everything is a nail' (Maslow, 1966, p. 15) – in certain practices or discourses we have become overdependent on particular tools, or indeed concepts, and we fail to see other possibilities. This means that when we make use of particular concepts to illuminate particular phenomena or contexts, those concepts also always screen other phenomena or contexts from view. Moreover, some important notions easily migrate from one field of knowledge to another: they are 'travelling concepts', a term used by cultural historian Mieke Bal. In her writings in the early 2000s, Bal studied concepts that were then important in many fields in the humanities – such as 'narrative', 'meaning' and 'myth' – to show how these notions changed when they travelled from one discipline to another (Bal, 2002). From the contributors to this *Vademecum*, who come from a broad range of disciplines and are based in different European countries, we have gathered a wealth of concepts that migrate and change their tunes when used in different settings. When it comes to the material context, architects and urbanists might discuss this process as a question of appropriateness in a given situation – of decorum – giving rise to the question: how can our understanding of urban places be enriched by the travels of theoretical concepts between different disciplinary and geographical locations? Moreover, how do concepts change when used in different geographical, cultural, disciplinary or linguistic contexts? We asked scholars from the Writing Urban Places network and beyond to contribute terms they considered relevant in their own fields and approaches to the study of urban places, and we have brought them together in this publication. The collection is not a finite project, but something more like a design exercise: the process of thinking, writing, discussing and editing these texts became the result itself, trying to map out the horizon of what 'minor' can mean within the concrete framework of the network.

Overall, our approach was to try to avoid 'major' terms that are generally shared – such as 'public space', 'collectivity' or 'sustainability' – and to seek less obvious terms that may migrate productively among disciplines. We considered it fruitful to investigate the local, and possibly the alternative, the disenfranchised or the overlooked: the minor. Minor terms can be major within one frame of reference, or commonly used in ordinary language, but become minor when smuggled into the discourse of urbanism, and this is how we have approached the exercise here. We also chose to include

terms not only from academic realms, but also from professional, artistic or activist realms that address urban places.
The term 'minor' can be seen in the light of our ambition to look at the local and social specificity of urban places, and to challenge established discursive frameworks by giving voice to multiple actors in the debate. In our exploration of minor concepts, we refer to a number of sources where the idea of the minor has been discussed – particularly in relation to literature and architecture, two fields that our network brings together.

Minor literature, minor architecture

The term 'minor' is taken from French philosophers Gilles Deleuze and Félix Guattari, who used the term 'minor literature' in their book *Kafka: Toward a minor literature* (1975/1986). They describe the work of the author Franz Kafka, who lived in Prague and wrote in German as part of a German-speaking Bohemian Jewish minority. German was a minority language in Prague, but not in the Austro-Hungarian Empire to which Prague belonged until it became the capital of Czechoslovakia in 1918. The literature Kafka wrote thus made a minoritarian use of the German language, altering it in the process. In this way, Kafka's writing transgressed the boundaries of mainstream literature, both in his choice of topics and in his actual use of language. In many cases, such minor literature – which comes from social groups who might be seeking alternatives to their marginal positions in society – offers imaginings of new potential situations: 'if the writer is in the margins or off to the side of his or her fragile community, that situation puts him or her that much more in a position to express another potential community, to forge the means of another consciousness and another sensibility' (Deleuze & Guattari, 1975/1986, p. 17). As literary theorist Ronald Bogue has argued, minor literature – i.e. literature written in the context of cultural and linguistic minorities – often involves a particular appropriation of language, as well as the construction of imagined alternative realities

(Bogue, 2003, pp. 91–114). Consequently, this raises the possibility that such specific and appropriative literary accounts of urban places might be useful in revealing those places' societal issues and architectural specificities. While Deleuze and Guattari apply the term to literature, in our understanding 'minor' can also relate to any form of discourse that creates its own discursive territory: not only literature, but also art and theory can be used in a minor way to challenge existing normative frameworks. Each theoretical domain develops a form of discursive language that is important to its interpretative task. The downside of such domain-specific jargon is that concepts may start to function as shibboleths – that is, words (or ways to pronounce or spell them) that are used to differentiate the members of a specific group from outsiders. In academic disciplines, a shibboleth can be a concept that allows someone to determine who is an 'expert' and has a right to speak with authority, and who is not and must therefore be explicitly or implicitly silenced. In some cases, discursive language becomes tribalist: it can only be understood by those in the same discursive tribe. It is this form of discursive hegemony that the notion of the minor allows us to challenge: one might be well versed in a specific domain, but the complexity of the city requires the conceptual complexity of different frameworks, including regional differences and sensitivities.

One can therefore argue that the use of minor concepts forces the researcher to pay extra attention to this messy, contextual and situated aspect of every urban analysis. A minor use of a majority's language implies, as Deleuze and Guattari argue, an 'underdevelopment', a 'willed poverty' (Deleuze & Guattari, 1975/1986, pp. 18–19). But it also enables an intensification of the language used: partial readings, and even misreadings, can be productive. Precisely such modifications to a major discourse create unexpected and intense encounters with other domains of knowledge, establishing strange hybrids, and offering possibilities to link theory with practice, politics and art.

Architect Jill Stoner has defined 'minor architecture' as architecture that emerges from the bottom of dominant power structures and works from the specific – that which is perceived as obsolete and celebrates contingency (Stoner, 2012). She writes that Deleuze and Guattari defined minor literature by coining three terms that are now so widely used as to have become major, at least in certain areas of cultural theory: 'deterritorialisation', 'politicisation' and 'collective enunciation': 'In architecture as in literature, these traits exist in multiplicities, as both figurative and literal mechanisms, as both acts and consequences. But such multiplicities are deceptively light; they do not produce an excess' (Stoner, 2012, pp. 3–4).
If the urban forms of contemporary capitalist urban structures feed off potentially endless growth, and thus have continuous lateral expansion as their main horizon of expectation, we may see minor terms as a way of counteracting that order of excess. That which is minor may creep in from behind the scenes, in places where we least expect it. Using, debating, arguing over and taking the minor terms of this *Vademecum* into these cities, we hope, may thus unveil some of these relationships. As Stoner writes:

The spatial conditions we are calling minor may already be close by, latent within our consumer objects, veiled by property relations. To tease them out is to think outside conventional visual paradigms, to resist the linearity of time and the seduction of progress. The study of minor architectures is itself a study in architectural kinships – but not those derived from geographical responsiveness (regionalism), aesthetic canons (style), or program-driven institutions (typology). Instead, it uncovers a shared spatial code that transcends conventional categories, ensuring that minor architectures will always operate through complex multiplicities. (Stoner, 2012, pp. 15–16).

A collective project

Deleuze and Guattari stress in their book that this notion of the minor is always political and related to a collective. The same goes for this *Vademecum*, which is in a real sense an assemblage of different domains, different voices. It is a collective enunciation of different forms of knowledge. As Stoner notes in her book *Toward a minor architecture*, Deleuze and Guattari begin another of their co-written works, *A Thousand Plateaus*, with the following statement: 'The two of us wrote *Anti-Oedipus* together. Since each of us was several, there was already quite a crowd'; Stoner goes on to state that 'they thus neatly write themselves out of the authorial superiority that characterizes the very philosophical tradition that they argue against' (Stoner, 2012, p. 76). It is from a similar place of concern and opportunity, that we have embarked on this book project as an experiment in bringing together a plurality of voices in very short texts on minor concepts – and as an experiment in co-writing, as in this introduction – with the goal of sharing and combining knowledge, thereby breaking apart the major narrative voice of the expert or authority in order to create a more differentiated one. We are aware that there is a fundamental but also potentially awkward gesture in making 'minor' the leading and thus even major term of a project, albeit with the aim of challenging the very notion of the major.

Of course, there is a paradox in our referencing two of the most famous male philosophers of the elitist and privileged French academic tradition – authors who brought their voices together to challenge the notion of the singular academic author, and indeed Western culture's understanding of the subject and subjectivity as major constructs. We also realise that since we are scholars who work with abstract theoretical knowledge, and who are part of a privileged international academic world, the discourse we evoke has to work very hard to establish real links with the surrounding world. Yet a main outcome of the *Vademecum* as an exercise is the way the terms and voices vacillate between major and minor, abstract and concrete, situated and theoretical, practice and academia. As the Writing Urban Places network includes scholars and practitioners engaged in fieldwork in a variety of European cities, we hope this *Vademecum* will become a field guide to bring theoretical concepts into investigations in real urban places and to formulate other concepts based on the encounter with those places.

A field guide

It is our wish that the *Vademecum* should be used as a companion with which to explore the city. While the metropolis dominates much of contemporary urban culture in Asia and the Americas, Europe is predominantly populated by a relatively even spread of medium-sized cities (Dehaene et al., 2013). These cities are highly significant for European urban lives and narratives, but they seem to be minor in much urban writing, whether literary or scholarly (Benne , 2018). They have often been overlooked in mainstream urban discourse, which in past decades has foregrounded the metropolis and concepts such as 'the generic city' (Koolhaas, 1995/1997; Musch, 2001, pp. 2–8). However, the fact that medium-sized cities are often important regional centres, offering cultural, institutional and social facilities to a wider area, is an important starting point for our COST Action network. With this project we explore whether these minor terms could be taken into the field by means of this *Vademecum*, to inspire new perspectives on the intricate social and spatial conditions of urban places. We hope that the theoretical concepts collected in this *Vademecum* will inspire spatial professionals, researchers, students and communities to exchange knowledge, to engage with urban places and to discover and develop responsible approaches to current urban challenges.
From the beginning, the work in this project was envisioned to be an open and inclusive process where we could pool and build on the existing energies of the many participants in the Writing Urban Places network. Being a European group, we are able to draw on knowl-

edge not only from different disciplines but also from different geographical places, from Lithuania to Portugal and Croatia. The project of gathering minor concepts for writing urban places is a potentially endless endeavour. We hope that the *Vademecum* will inspire a continued exploration of how other minor concepts might contribute to our understanding of urban narratives in the future. Not aspiring to be a comprehensive list or glossary, this book lists the concepts alphabetically rather than thematically, allowing the reader to interrelate them in many ways. Selecting and combining terms has been an intuitive and shared exercise, and we editors thank all of the contributors to this publication for their time and dedication – and the EU's COST network funding for allowing us to meet in person as much as in writing. Our collaborative process ultimately produced precisely seventy seven minor terms, but this is an arbitrary number that may be revised, expanded or reduced in future work. It simply captures a particular moment in the ongoing process of sharing knowledge and perspectives that takes place within the network.
But if the *Vademecum* is to become operative as a field guide – and if the project is to be feasible as a book – we hope that you will welcome this positively incomplete selection that we have made, and that you will take it with you into concrete urban contexts, add other interesting minor concepts, and explore their potential to create change towards more responsible, socially inclusive and locally specific urban places.

Further readings

Bal, M. (2002). *Travelling concepts in the humanities: A rough guide.* University of Toronto Press.

Benne, C. (2018). *Changing the story: The rise of the small city.* Carlsberg Foundation. https://www.carlsbergfondet.dk/en/Forskningsaktiviteter/Bevillingsstatistik/Bevillingsoversigt/CF18_0153_Christian-Benne

Bogue, R. (2003). *Deleuze on literature.* Routledge.

Dehaene, M., Notteboom, B., & Havik, K. (2013). *OASE 89: Medium: The mid-size city as a European condition and strategy.* NAI.

Deleuze, G., & Guattari, F. (1986), *Kafka: Toward a minor literature.* University of Minnesota Press. (Original work published 1975)

Koolhaas, R. (1997). Generic city. In: OMA, R. Koolhaas & B. Mau, *S, M, L, XL* (pp. 1239–1264). Taschen. (Original work published 1995)

Maslow, A. H. (1966). *The psychology of science: A reconnaissance.* Harper & Row.

Musch, M. (2001). Editorial. InMusch, M. and Schreurs, E.(Ed.), *OASE 54: Re: Generic City* (pp. 2–8). NAI.

Stoner, J. (2012). *Toward a minor architecture.* MIT Press.

Dalia Milián Bernal
Tampere University
Architecture
dalia.milianbernal@tuni.fi

Further readings

de Sola-Morales, I. (1995). Terrain vague. In Territorios (pp. 123–132). Gustavo Gili.

DeSilvey, C., & Edensor, T. (2013). Reckoning with ruins. Progress in Human Geography, 37(4), 465–485. https://doi.org/10.1177/0309132512462271

Macdonell, J. (1899). Occupation and 'res nullius'. Journal of the Society of Comparative Legislation, 1(2), 276–286.

Sassen, S. (2014). Expulsions. Harvard University Press.

Abandonment

The concept of *abandonment* refers to the action of surrendering something to another, or the condition of being renounced, given up completely, left entirely, forsaken. People, animals, things, property, actions, processes and responsibilities can be in a state of abandonment. Here, we focus on abandonment in the built environment, especially regarding urban property rights and the use of land. In Roman law, abandoned property is referred to as *derelict* property, meaning that the owner has purposely left the property with no intention of return (Macdonell, 1899). Thus, the abandoned property becomes ownerless, a *res nullius* that belongs to nobody and can therefore be owned by anybody.

The abandonment of buildings has been taking place for centuries, from Mayan pyramids to Second World War defence structures, from empty factories to abandoned shops and schools in declining towns. However, in no era has abandonment been as pervasive as it is in the contemporary city, where vacancy proliferates in parallel with urban growth. In the current state of neoliberal urbanisation, vacancy and abandonment seem to be structural, induced processes (Sassen, 2014). They materialise as deindustrialisation, land speculation, foreclosures, ecological crises and wars. Abandoned unfinished buildings fill the landscape in Spain, while newly constructed housing estates stand empty in Mexico.

Nonetheless, abandonment does not go unchallenged. In a constant critique of the system, buildings are occupied and laws amended, transforming abandoned properties into spaces of hope and social justice (DeSilvey & Edensor, 2013). European cities and towns contain plenty of these signs of social action and innovation.

Lars Frers
University of South-Eastern Norway
Social Science and Qualitative Methods
lars.frers@usn.no

Further readings

Bille, M., Hastrup, F., & Sørensen, T. F. (Eds). (2010). *An anthropology of absence: Materializations of transcendence and loss*. Springer.

Frers, L. (2013). The matter of absence. *Cultural Geographies, 20*(4), 431–445. https://doi.org/10.1177/1474474013477775

Gallagher, M. (2015). Sounding ruins: Reflections on the production of an 'audio drift'. *Cultural Geographies, 22*(3), 467–485. https://doi.org/10.1177/1474474014542745

Parr, H., Stevenson, O., Fyfe, N., & Woolnough, P. (2015). Living absence: The strange geographies of missing people. *Environment and Planning D: Society and Space, 33*(2), 191–208. https://doi.org/10.1068/d14080p

Absence

Urban places are defined not only by what and who is present in them, but also by what and who is absent. *Absence* has become a relevant term in research on place, especially in anthropology and geography (Bille et al., 2010; Frers, 2013). In these discourses, the term is mainly used in two different but related contexts. The term *absence* evokes phenomena that are beyond the material. Research on ghost towns, ruins and haunted places are good examples of this. Such research delves into the realm of the spectral as opposed to the material, as something that disturbs established notions of place and points to fissures and breakages in the urban structure. Another way of using the term is in contexts that centre on embodied experience (Frers, 2013). Here, absences arise in the experience of people for whom a concrete place, site, thing or person evokes memories and imaginings rooted in their prior bodily experience.

The term *trace* is relevant in both contexts, as it points to specific manifestations that establish a connection between what is there and what is missing (Parr et al., 2015). Absences, or experiences of absence, can be produced systematically, as is the case in most museums, in graveyards, and in heritage sites in general. Concrete experiences of absence can emerge in relation to war memorials and industrial ruins, which have different qualities for different individuals or social groups. However, absences can also arise suddenly and unexpectedly, based on individual and unplanned encounters. Some researchers give special attention to the senses and to how urban places are felt, taking sound, smell and touch into account as much as vision and movement (e.g. Gallagher, 2015). Narratives of absence can thus point to the emotional underbelly of the urban – to things that are forgotten but still there, more present for some than for others.

Willie Vogel
Delft University of Technology
Architecture
willie.c.vogel@gmail.com

Further readings

Greimas, A. J. (1987). Actants, actors, and figures. In *On meaning: Selected writings in semiotic theory* (pp. 106–120). University of Minnesota Press.

Latour, B. (1990). On actor-network theory: A few clarifications plus more than a few complications. *Philosophia, 25*, 47–64.

Actant

The word *actant* was first used in semiotics by the structuralist theorist Algirdas Greimas, who deployed it to analyse the character roles embedded in a story. He created a model in which, along three axis, six structural elements were set out: the actants. The model is like a pairing system in which two opposing actants work to form the story and refer to the interrelationships between all the stories' structural elements. The model initiated by Greimas enables to theoretically analyse actions within stories and can uncover ambiguities within the narrative.

More recently, the French philosopher Bruno Latour has used the word in his actor-network theory. In this theory, which is a plea for a broader conception of nature, Latour uses 'actant' to refer to both human and non-human actors. Replacing the word 'actor' with 'actant' reduces the dominance of human agency behind our current societal structure. An actant is something that acts on something else, creating a huge network of assemblages in which non-human things also work on us and actively shape us. Actor-network theory strives for more consciousness at the level of contexts and patterns within society.

These two slightly different usages of the term 'actant' both seem to address interrelationships within narratives about societies. For research into urban places, the concept of the actant offers a perspective in which both human and non-humans are actors that play roles in the integral structures of local urban narratives.

Ann Petermans, Jan Vanrie,
Ruth Stevens
Hasselt University
Faculty of Architecture & Arts
ann.petermans@uhasselt.be
jan.vanrie@uhasselt.be
ruth.stevens@uhasselt.be

Further readings

Gibson, J. (1979). *The ecological approach to visual perception*. Houghton Mifflin: Boston.

Morrison, A. (2014). Facebook and coaxed affordances. In A. Poletti & J. Rak (Eds), *Identity technologies: Constructing the self online* (pp. 112–131). The University of Wisconsin Press: Madison.

Rietveld, E., & Kiverstein, J. (2014). A rich landscape of affordances. *Ecological Psychology, 26*(4), 325–352.

Stevens, R., Petermans, A., & Vanrie, J. (forthcoming). Design for human flourishing in architecture: A theoretical framework to design spatial flourishing affordances. *Journal of Architectural and Planning Research*.

Affordance

The term *affordance* originates from psychology, where Gibson (1979) focused on exploring how particular resources in an environment, which can be picked up somewhat instinctively by a user in that environment, can offer possibilities for action that help to fulfil basic biological needs. Over the years, this interpretation of affordance has evolved to include affective and sociocultural aspects, implying the need for a fit between a person and the affordances that (s)he detects in an environment. As the concept of affordances has also become applied to technology (which increasingly contributes to the shaping of the environments where users spend time, e.g. the use of Facebook or Instagram), the 'action possibilities' for users can also be considered to have changed (Morrison, 2014).

The concept of affordances can be used to investigate how various kinds of environments, ranging from urban and public places to intimate interior spaces, appeal to particular users, and why they do so in different ways for different people.

Mirza Emirhafizović
University of Sarajevo
Political Sciences
mirza.emirhafizovic@fpn.unsa.ba

Further readings

Plouffe, L., & Kalache, A. (2010). Towards global age-friendly cities: Determining urban features that promote active aging. *Journal of Urban Health, 87*(5), 733–739. https://doi.org/10.1007/s11524-010-9466-0

Walsh, K., Scharf, T., & Keating, N. (2016). Social exclusion of older persons: A scoping review and conceptual framework. *European Journal of Ageing, 14*(1), 81–98. https://doi.org/10.1007/s10433-018-0483-2

WHO. (2007). *Global age-friendly cities: A guide.* WHO.

Age-friendly city

Given that urbanisation and population ageing are happening simultaneously in Europe today, researchers and policymakers are concerned with the increasing proportion of senior citizens (i.e. those aged 65 years and above) and how their diverse and specific needs can be respected (Plouffe & Kalache, 2010; World Health Organisation (WHO), 2007). Consequently, providing all the necessary conditions to ensure active ageing is one of the top priorities in many cities.

The concept of the *age-friendly city* was developed by the WHO in 2007 to enhance the quality of life of older adults. It is closely linked to reducing the social exclusion of older persons (Walsh et al., 2016). In order to make visible progress towards the age-friendly city, the WHO has recommended that services and structures should be improved in the following domains: outdoor spaces and buildings, transport, housing, social participation, respect and social inclusion, civic participation and employment, communication and information, community support and health services (WHO 2007).

In Europe, urban narratives around ageing have been gaining more relevance since the turn of the century. Storying ageing in the city might bring nuance and depth to discussions and thinking about cities, notably in terms of raising awareness of ageing in the city and possibly creating appropriate policy measures to respond to it.

Jana Čulek
Delft University of Technology
Architecture
J.Culek@tudelft.nl

Further readings

Bycanck, V. (Ed.) (2005). *Superstudio: The Middelburg lectures.* De Vleeshal & Zeeuws Museum.

Lang, P., & Menking, W. (2003). *Superstudio: Life without objects.* Skira Editore.

Robinson, K. S. (2018). Dystopias now. https://communemag.com/dystopias-now/

Anti-utopia

Anti-utopia is a term that appears at various points in time throughout utopian discourse. Even though the commonest definition of anti-utopias links them directly to dystopias, given that they are seen as an opposite to the 'good place' (*eu-topos* in ancient Greek), the meaning ascribed to the term has changed during the last century. Emerging in the field of architecture in the 1960s, and commonly connected to the work of the Italian architectural group Superstudio, the term has taken on a more critical role in utopian discourse. The science fiction writer Kim Stanley Robinson (2018) explains, through the use of the semiotic square (a tool used for analysing relationships between concepts through their oppositions), that every concept has both its not (dystopia) and its anti (anti-utopia), and that the two differ significantly. While dystopia envisions ways in which things could get worse, anti-utopia offers a critique of the notion of utopia itself: it implies that 'the idea of utopia itself is wrong and bad, and that any attempt to try to make things better is sure to wind up making things worse' (Robinson, 2018). Anti-utopias can therefore be used as a critical method for reflecting on society, without the need to escape to an idealised utopian narrative where all issues have been resolved, or to a dystopian one where all has gone awry. By acknowledging the flaws and shortcomings of utopias and exploiting them, anti-utopias propose critical reflections on society where the goal is not betterment or fear, but rather a re-examination and questioning of the status quo through imaginative means.

Adriana Martins
Universidade Católica Portuguesa
Culture Studies
adrimartins@fch.lisboa.ucp.pt

Arcade. In J. S. Curl (Ed.), *A Dictionary of Architecture and Landscape Architecture* (2nd ed.). Oxford University Press. https://www.oxfordreference.com/view/10.1093/acref/9780198606789.001.0001/acref-9780198606789-e-238

Benjamin, W. (1999). *The arcades project.* Belknap Press.

Benjamin, W. (2019). *As passagens de Paris.* Assírio & Alvim.

Moore, B. (2016). Walter Benjamin and *The arcades project.* In J. Tambling (Ed.), *The Palgrave handbook of literature and the city* (pp. 59–73). Palgrave Macmillan.

Arcades

Assuming diverse styles and functions over time, *arcades* have shaped the urban fabric and expressed cultural habits, forms of social interaction, economic structures and trade relationships. In the 19th century, arcades were glass- and iron-covered shopping streets that epitomised the experience of the modern bourgeois city, urban renewal and transformation. As lively spaces of conviviality and entertainment, 19th-century arcades were the forerunners of department stores.
Arcades were also a literary trope, demonstrating that writing and cities are inseparable (Moore, 2016). Perhaps the best example is German philosopher Walter Benjamin's *The Arcades Project*, which analyses how arcades revolutionised Parisian life at economic, social and cultural levels in the 19th and early 20th centuries. This long and complex essay illustrates how the city can be written and questioned, and it has become a major reference point for any attempt to write urban spaces. In his introduction to his own Portuguese translation of the work, Benjamin scholar João Barrento considers the arcades as a paradigm of the city. They were the space where new forms of trade, architectural changes brought about by the use of glass and iron, and developments in photography and optics, among others, took place. The arcades thus represented a microcosm of the city, and of 19th-century civilisation and culture.

Eliana Sousa Santos
Universidade de Coimbra
Architecture
e.sousasantos@gmail.com

Further readings

Picon, A. (2000). Anxious landscapes: From the ruin to rust. *Grey Room, 1*, 64–83. https://doi.org/10.1162/152638100750173065

Roger, A. (1997). *Court traité du paysage.* Gallimard.

Sebald, W. G. (2000). *Vertigo.* Harvill Press. (Original work published 1990)

Artialisation

Philosopher Alain Roger (1997) coined the concept of *artialisation* to refer to the transformation of landscapes through culture. In fact, he refers to double artialisation, that is, two types of mediation of landscapes through art: *in situ* and *in visu* (Roger, 1997, p. 16). In the case of artialisation *in situ*, the transformation of the territory occurs directly, via a material intervention such as an architectural structure, monument or artwork. The second type of artialisation, *in visu*, is 'more economical and more sophisticated' (Roger, 1997, p. 17), since in this case the territory is mediated indirectly through its representation in works of art, literature or history

For Roger, the example of Sainte-Victoire mountain in Aix-en-Provence is a paradigm of double artialisation thanks to its representations by the artist Cézanne. Quoting the painter Charles Lapicque, Roger argues that the 'countryside of Aix-en-Provence [resembles] a Cézanne' while the mountain itself 'ends up becoming a Cézanne' (Roger, 1997, p. 21). Hence, this territory was changed by Cézanne in both ways: artialisation *in visu* (in Cézanne's paintings) become artialisation *in situ* (the mountain itself), where several trails aim to recreate the walks and views that Cézanne explored.

A more recent example of this dynamic between artialisation *in visu* and *in situ* can be found in Sebaldweg, the trail dedicated to the German writer W. G. Sebald close to his home town of Wertach-im-Allgäu. This trail recreates Sebald's walk as described in his novel *Vertigo* (1990/2000), and it includes several plaques in key locations referred in the text. In this case, the artialisation *in visu* created by the novel has also contributed to the artialisation *in situ* defined by the trail.

Following Roger, the architect Antoine Picon appropriated the concept of artialisation to describe cityscapes rather than the countryside. Picon finds that Roger's double artialisation – that is, 'the apprehension of the environment and the interpretation of the characteristics of that environment through the resources of art' (Picon, 2000, p. 69) – to be especially relevant for the analysis of the contemporary city, since the character of today's 'cityscape originates more from an overabundance of aesthetic intentions than from their radical absence' (Picon, 2000, p. 69).

Klaske Havik
Delft University of Technology
Architecture
K.M.Havik@tudelft.nl

Further readings

Böhme, G. (2006). *Architektur und Atmosphäre.* Wilhelm Fink.

Böhme, G., Griffero, T., & Thibaud, J.-P. (2014). *Architecture and atmosphere.* Tapio Wirkkala-Rut Bryk Foundation.

Havik, K. (2018). Writing urban atmospheres. In J. Charley (Ed.), *Research companion to architecture, literature and the city* (pp. 270–282). Routledge.

Havik, K., Tielens, G., & Teerds, H. (Eds) (2013). *OASE 91: Building atmosphere.* NAi Publishers.

Pérez-Gómez, A. (2016). *Attunement: Architectural meaning after the crisis of modern science.* MIT Press.

Atmosphere

To address the social and local specificities of urban places, the term *atmosphere* can be productive. As the coming together of objective, spatial and material arrangements and the embodied, perceiving subject (Böhme, 2006), 'atmosphere' is a crucial notion to conceptualise the complex affective relations between citizens and urban places. Strangely, the concept was rather absent from architectural and urban discourse in the 20th century. Atmosphere is essentially ambiguous, always mediating between different aspects. It is therefore difficult to address atmosphere with conventional analytical tools such as maps, plans and sections, or to discuss it in the rational terms that prevailed under functionalist approaches to architecture and urban planning.

In descriptions of architecture in novels, stories and poems, however, atmosphere is often eloquently brought to the fore. Urban narratives have the capacity to offer 'attuned' relationships between people and places (Pérez-Gómez, 2016), as well as between different individuals. If writers and poets are able to capture atmospheres in their work, literary descriptions of urban places may provide information for architects, urban planners and researchers to understand the atmospheric possibilities of place.

Juan A. García-Esparza
Universitat Jaume I
Architectural Conservation
juan.garcia@uji.es

Further readings

Fairclough, G. (2012). A prospect of time: Interactions between landscape architecture and archaeology. In S. Bell, I. S. Herlin & R. Stiles (Eds), *Exploring the boundaries of landscape architecture* (pp. 83–114). Routledge.

García-Esparza, J. A. (2018). Are World Heritage concepts of integrity and authenticity lacking in dynamism? A critical approach to Mediterranean auto-topic landscapes. *Landscape Research, 43*(6), 817–830.

Autotopia

Autotopia refers to spatial practices where the role of the non-expert is emphasised – where ordinary residents participate in the intellectual and material construction of places. This is slightly different from the role of the architectural historian, and it transcends the contemporary conceptualisation of urban conservation. Autotopias encompass transformation, abandonment and decay, as well as the technical ingenuity born of necessity and adaptation. In terms of conservation, an autotopian place is slightly dangerous, but exciting and somehow democratic. Nowadays, autotopias are considered by Unesco to be threats, as their dynamic character is opposed to the static mechanisms of control and effective protection. Autotopias give priority to the recomposition of cultural processes, thereby allowing inhabitants to maintain both the material and social construction of place. This dialectical process may achieve the material and social continuity of cultural heritage. In turn, this correlated continuity can be effectively built on the idea of a contemporary process of assemblage rather than on the idea of preservation disengaged from present time.

Kris Pint
Hasselt University
Faculty of Architecture & Arts
kris.pint@uhasselt.be

Further readings

Pint, K. (2012). The avatar as a methodological tool for the embodied exploration of virtual environments. *CLC Web, 14*(3). http://docs.lib.purdue.edu/clcweb/vol14/iss3/3/

Ryan, M.-L. (2001). *Narrative as virtual reality: Immersion and interactivity in literature and electronic media.* Johns Hopkins University Press.

Avatar

Avatar is a term originating from cyberpunk. One of its uses is in game design, where it refers to the 'incarnation' of the player through a character in the game world. This notion can also be used in the analysis of environments that cannot be accessed by the researcher – for example, if the environment in question is restricted, demolished or imaginary. Since the sense of embodiment is a crucial aspect of spatial (and urban) experience, an avatar can be used to describe embodied immersion in a specific (virtual) space in order to explore it affectively and/or sensorially. The notion is particularly useful for 'writing urban places' because it enables the researcher to engage seriously with the complex affective and sensual aspects of a specific urban environment.

Sonja Novak
Josip Juraj Strossmayer University of Osijek
Humanities
snovak@ffos.hr

Further readings

Kaern, M., Phillips, B.S., Cohen, Robert S. (Eds). (1990). *Georg Simmel and contemporary sociology*. Kluwer Academic.

Simmel, G. (1903). Die Grossstadt. In T. Petermann (Ed.), *Vorträge und Aufsätze zur Städteausstellung: Jahrbuch der Gehe-Stiftung* (pp. 185–206). Zahn & Jaensch.

Simmel, G. (2006). *Die Großstädte und das Geistesleben*. Suhrkamp.

Blasiertheit

Georg Simmel (1858–1918), a German philosopher and founder of urban sociology, introduced the term *Blasiertheit* in his collection of essays *The Metropolis and Mental Life* (1903). Often translated into English as 'blasé attitude', *Blasiertheit* is an attitude and aptitude of city dwellers whose psychology has been altered by the city itself. In his works on the industrialised metropolis at the turn of the twentieth century, Simmel drew on his own experience as city dweller in Berlin to analyse the differences between rural and city life and the influence of the city on the individual. According to Simmel, city dwellers must confront the ever-changing environment on an everyday basis, and over time this makes them immune, numb or indifferent to the stimuli around them. He argues that the mental state of city dwellers is completely different from that of inhabitants in smaller, rural settlements, because city dwellers need to quickly adjust to changes that reflect the abundance of impulses comprising life in a large urban area.

Since the city and its development are based on finances, exchange and currency, city dwellers are able to establish meaningful connections only with this financial aspect of modern life; this further contributes to their ability to develop defence mechanisms that help them contend with the city's numerous stimuli. *Blasiertheit*, according to Simmel, is an unconscious survival strategy of city dwellers. It can thus be argued that the city should be understood not only as something that surrounds us and is there for us to utilise, but also as a human-made phenomenon that has an effect on our inner lives, changing our psyche and our attitudes towards our surroundings. This realisation raises questions about how an individual reflects the city itself – for example, it opens up possibilities for the analysis of an author's or character's attitude and state of mind in urban narratives.

Adriana Martins
Universidade Católica Portuguesa
Culture Studies
adrimartins@fch.lisboa.ucp.pt

Further readings

Genpei, A. (2010). *Hyperart: Thomasson.* Kaya Press.

AFP (2011, 21 August). Rise and fall of the boot-scraper. *Independent.* https://www.independent.co.uk/property/house-and-home/rise-and-fall-of-the-boot-scraper-2341628.html

Trufelman, A. (2014, 26 August). *Thomassons.* 99% Invisible. https://99percentinvisible.org/episode/thomassons/

Boot scraper

A *boot scraper* is a cast-iron object that can take various shapes. In major world cities such as London and New York in the 18th and 19th centuries, boot scrapers were placed outside some houses to remove excrement and dirt from people's boots. According to historian Christian Loir, boot scrapers are key to urban history, as they are part of the history of walking in the city (AFP 2011). In European cities, until the late 18th century, only the poor walked in the streets. This habit changed when walking became fashionable and the elite discovered the city, thereby granting public space new quality and value. As more people adopted the walking habit, boot scrapers changed social customs: people started to remove their shoes before going indoors, and manuals began to be published to explain how to be civil by not taking off one's shoes. Although boot scrapers can be seen as forerunners of today's doormats, they can also be considered 'Thomassons' (Genpei, 2010), that is, leftovers or vestiges of the past that no longer serve any discernible purpose in the urban fabric but are maintained nonetheless (Trufelman, 2014). Boot scrapers are thus historical traces that 'write' the urban space from social and cultural perspectives.

Henriette Steiner
University of Copenhagen
Landscape, Architecture and Planning
hst@ign.ku.dk

Kristin Veel
University of Copenhagen
Arts and Cultural Studies
kristinv@hum.ku.dk

Further readings

Steiner, H., & Veel, K. (2020). *Tower to tower: Gigantism in architecture and digital culture.* MIT Press.

Weiser, M. (1991). The computer for the 21st century. *Scientific American*, 265(3), 94–104.

Calmness

Calmness derives from 'calm technology', a phrase suggested by computer scientist Mark Weiser (1952–1999) of the Palo Alto-based research lab Xerox PARC. As one of the founding researchers into ubiquitous computing in the early 1990s, Weiser used the word 'calm' to describe technologies that integrate seamlessly into our everyday lives without calling attention to themselves: 'The most profound technologies are those that disappear. They weave themselves into the fabric of everyday life until they are indistinguishable from it', he wrote in 1991 in a short text titled 'The computer for the 21st century'. At that time, Weiser and his colleague John Seely Brown saw the emergence of the Internet as establishing a paradigm of distributed computing on a large scale. They envisioned that this would mark a shift to a networked technology distributed across many platforms and large distances. Regardless of the scale at which they functioned, these connecting technologies would operate in a way that was largely invisible to the user, whether because they were hidden from view, very small or spread over large distances. Through their ubiquitous integrated and semi-automatic functioning, such technologies would recede into the background of everyday life: hence their characterisation as calm.

In recent years, with the widespread use of smartphones and the digital embedment of technologies – for example, in relation to urban transport, from digital wayfinding technologies and maps to parking apps, the tracking of electric cars or e-scooters, and digital payment systems in public transport services – it seems as if we are moving in the direction that Weiser and Brown foresaw as a shift to calm technologies. These are examples of a largely invisible form of distributed computing on a large scale, seamlessly tracking, following and augmenting our lives in the city. Since these technologies often operate outside out direct field of attention, narratives can be a tool to approach the workings and effects of these technologies and how they concern our affective relationships with other people and the physical fabric of the city.

This entry is based on material published in Steiner and Veel (2020).

Klaske Havik
Delft University of Technology
Architecture
K.M.Havik@tudelft.nl

Willie Vogel
Delft University of Technology
Architecture
willie.c.vogel@gmail.com

Further readings

Haraway, D. J. (2016). *Staying with the trouble: Making kin in the Chthulucene.* Duke University Press.

Le Guin, U. K. (1986). The carrier bag theory of fiction. In *Dancing at the edge of the world* (pp. 149 - 154). Grove Press.

Carrier bag

Stories give us the ability to focalise underlying emotions, and to imagine real and possible situations. The philosopher and fiction writer Ursula K. Le Guin (1986) uses the metaphor of the *carrier bag* to refer to the way stories are composed and collected: this bag, from which you take things and into which you also put things, is a recipient – like its beholder. Le Guin explains that being a recipient can be a tool to start new imaginings and relationships. According to Le Guin, the conventional perspective of heroic, triumphant, technological and male-dominated literature can be radically reversed if we consider the carrier bag as humanity's first tool: a tool for gathering food and carrying the basic necessities of life. This perspective is a more communal, caregiving one which leads to another type of literature. From the carrier bag perspective, Le Guin describes fiction as:

A way of trying to describe what is in fact going on, what people actually do and feel, how people relate to everything else in this vast sack, this belly of the universe, this womb of things to be and tomb of things that were, this unending story. (Le Guin, 1986, p. 154)

The consequences of this perspective for architecture might take us away from the master-architect narrative or the idea that a work of architecture can be conceived of as having a single author. Instead, if each work of architecture is understood as a collection of different stories and perspectives, this less 'heroic' stance might enable other imaginaries of architecture by dealing with the question of the 'ordinary', and acknowledging the multitude of things – namely, stories and thoughts – it accommodates.

Nevena Daković
University of Arts, Belgrade
Film and Media Studies
n.m.dakovic@gmail.com

Further readings

Daković, N. (2011). Imagining Belgrade: The cultural/cinematic identity of a city on European fringes. In K. Pizzi & G. Weiss-Sussex (Eds), *The cultural identities of European cities* (pp. 61–77). Peter Lang.

Lefebvre, M. (Ed.). (2006). *Landscape and film*. Routledge.

Ryan, M., Kenneth, F., & Azaryahu, N. (2016). *Narrating space/spatializing narrative: Where narrative theory and geography meet*. Ohio State University Press.

Stam, R. (2000). *Film theory: An introduction*. Blackwell.

Cinematic cityscape

A *cinematic cityscape* is the landscape of a city as reflected and portrayed in films. With its privileged place in visual media – painting, photography, cinema and more – the cityscape has become a site for a variety of constructed meanings concerning urban developments, histories and identities. The investigation of the cinematic cityscape thus amounts to much more than the analysis of a narrative's urban spatial background. Cinematic cityscapes appear not only in movies that are explicitly about cities, but also in a large number of movies with urban settings in general. Hence, studying the cinematic cityscape means exploring the ways in which a cityscape is narrativised and mapped out; the ways it hybridises the real, present-day city, its past, and the imagined city of the future; and the modes in which fiction rubs up against facts, myths or previous representational traditions.
Film theorist Robert Stam (2000) conceptualises the link between cinema and cityscape as an ontological interdependence of time and space where a change in one register automatically entails changes in the other. The medium of moving images is a perfect example of the 'spatialisation of time and temporalisation of space', i.e. the conversion and representation of time in spatial terms, or conversely of space in temporal forms. The history of the city is inscribed in its cinematic space – images of streets, houses, sites etc. Conversely, spatial changes in the city, its de- and reconstructions, can be read from a temporal perspective, i.e. as revealing the temporalities of the city's development.
Making cinematic cityscapes can be understood as a specific practice of narrating urban places. Its specificity lies in the multi-media practice of combining images and sounds (visual and audio texts) in narratives that have emerged from written texts and which could also be transformed back into written texts. The shifts of format between written, audio and visual texts (screenplays, films, books) create a multisensorial, multimedia sense of time and space that is recognisable and readable as characteristic of the city.

Matthew Skjonsberg
ETH Zürich, Regional Design
and Landscape Architecture
skjonsberg@arch.ethz.ch

Further readings

Adshead, S. D. (1910). An introduction to civic design. *Town Planning Review, 1*(1), 3–17.

Arnsperger, C., & Skjonsberg, M. (2018). A civic hope: From Lausanne to Los Angeles. In M. Viganò (Ed.), *Urbanisme de l'espoir: Projeter des horizons d'attente* (pp. 53–74). Metis Presses.

Holford, W. (1949). Civic design: An inquiry into the scope and nature of town planning. *Town Planning Review, 20*(1), 17–31.

Skjonsberg, M. (2018). Civic design. In *A new look at civic design: Park systems in America* (pp. 357–406). [Thesis 8095, EPFL].

Civic design

Before the industrial agenda of 'urban design', which broadly promotes the economy and technology, there was the social agenda of *civic design*, which focuses on creating ecology and community. The 'world's first school of planning' was the School of Civic Design, founded in Liverpool in 1909 by sociologists, landscape architects and other associates of Patrick Geddes – a 'regional designer' and Britain's first ecologist. Within a year, similar programmes were established at the most advanced schools on both sides of the Atlantic, including Harvard University, where the civic design programme was established by none other than landscape architect Frederick Law Olmsted Jnr. The historical record shows that undertook to influence academics at several key institutions to abandon the use of the phrase 'civic design', to close programmes bearing that name, and to replace these with 'urban design' programmes (Skjonsberg, 2018). Among the first of these were Sigfried Giedion at MIT (1953), Josep Lluís Sert at Harvard (1954), Jane Jacobs at Columbia University (1955) and Kevin Lynch, also at MIT (1956).

A New Look at Civic Design was the working title for Lynch's research – eventually published as *Image of the City* (1960) – prior to his receiving funding from the corporate sponsors who were then actively dismantling civic design programmes in order to establish the urban design paradigm. Indeed, some contemporary scholars tend to portray these practices as equivalent – for example, retroactively branding 'civic designers' as 'urban designers' – but in fact the scope of civic design was always less commercial and more holistic than the contemporary practice of urban design, which still largely operates according to the logics of vested economic interests. In contrast to 'urbanism', any critical assessment of which reveals deep ties to colonialism – including the use of such urban-centric terminology as 'hinterlands' and 'peasants' to refer to citizens of rural settlements – civic design systematically relates nature and culture, rural and urban, young and old, rich and poor, top-down and bottom-up.

Katarzyna Kopecka-Piech
University of Wroclaw
Institute of Journalism and
Social Communication
katarzyna.kopecka.piech@gmail.com

Further readings

Gumpert G, Drucker S, 2007, "Mobile communication in the twenty-first century or "everybody, everywhere at any time", in Displacing place. Mobile Communication in the Twenty-first Century, Ed. K Sharon (Peter Lang, New York) pp. 7-20.

Kopecka-Piech K, 2012, Converging Media Spaces: Introducing an Emergent Field of Studies, „Studia Humanistyczne AGH", no 3, pp. 77-91.

Converging media spaces

Converging media spaces are hybrid spaces integrating elements of urban space and media space, which are a result of bidirectional integration and infiltration of media technologies (media infrastructures, devices, content and data) and elements of urban space (properties, infrastructures, institutions and data). They are the result of mediatization of cities and urbanization of media, that is on the one hand, the transformation of the city under the influence of media (e.g. adapting the facade of buildings to screens emitting media content), and on the other hand, the transformation of media due to their strong location in urban space, especially in large cities (e.g. the importance of location-based media technologies in mobile applications dedicated to smartphones). Converging media spaces are generated by convergent practices of new media technology users. They result in generating multiplied places and are characterised by blurred and unclear boundaries between physical and digital; public and private; commercial and non-commercial. "The mixed-use zones of modern urban environments embody convergence of media, convergence of electronic and media space, convergence of digital and physical presence, and convergence of public and private domains". (Gumpert & Drucker, 2007, p. 18). Contemporary cities are full of media technologies and data that cover them in many dimensions: material, digital, augmented, hybrid. From the other side media technologies (especially portable and ubiquitous) are filled with urban information and data in different formats. Mutual strengthening of both dimensions results in a synergy effects: socio-cultural, civic, commercial, artistic, etc. Moreover, they are subject to dynamic changes, and they are susceptible to destabilisation, and annihilation.

Tom Avermaete and Hans Teerds
ETH Zürich
History and Theory of Urban Design
tom.avermaete@gta.arch.ethz.ch and
hans.teerds@gta.arch.ethz.ch

Klaske Havik
Delft University of Technology
Architecture
K.M.Havik@tudelft.nl

Further readings

Avermaete, T., Teerds, H., Havik, K., Hernández, J. M., & Floet, W. W. (2016–2018). *Constructing the commons.* http://constructingthecommons.com/

Bollier, D., & Helfrich, S. (2012). *The wealth of the commons: A world beyond market and state.* Levellers Press.

Ostrom, E. (1990) *Governing the commons: The evolution of institutions for collective action.* Cambridge University Press.

Commons

The term *commons* historically refers to natural resources that we, the people, hold in common, resources that are the property of no individual and are available to all: air, water, earth. In medieval England and Central European countries, the commons were specific parcels of agricultural land intended for communal use. Nowadays, the city can be understood as the ultimate common socio-spatial resource, a collective cultural construct composed by and for its inhabitants.

Around the notion of the commons, a challenging field of thinking has emerged in economics and political and social sciences, suggesting radically different ways to organise our societies. Elinor Ostrom (1990) put forward the idea of the commons as a collective action that challenges existing perspectives on economics and policy. More recently, David Bollier and Silke Helfrich (2012) have used the commons as a model to think about the many domains of everyday life that lie beyond the dominant discourse of market economy and state intervention. In these theories, however, there is little notion of how architectural and urban spaces contribute to the formation of the commons.

From the perspective of architecture and urban design, the built environment appears to be a key element of the commons. Concrete and tangible architectural and urban figures (construction systems, spaces, buildings) can function as commons, as they represent an idea of commonality or organise communal practices. In addition, the commons can be looked upon from a procedural perspective, implying the rituals, pleasures and politics of cooperation that shape buildings and cities. This encompasses the shared effort of designers, advisers, constructors and owners, but architectural projects are also the result of the commonalities of other stakeholders, such as inhabitants, users and neighbours, who negotiate forces into a new venture.

Anne Margrethe Wagner
University of Copenhagen
Landscape Architecture and Planning
amw@ign.ku.dk

Further readings

de Certeau, M. (1988). *The practice of everyday life*. University of California Press. (Original work published 1984)

Levaco, R. (Ed.). (1974). *Kuleshov on film: Writings by Lev Vladimirovich Kuleshov*. University of California Press.

Wagner, A. M. (2016). Permitted exceptions: Authorised temporary urban spaces between vision and everyday. Department of Geosciences and Natural Resource Management, Faculty of Science, University of Copenhagen.

Creative geography

Creative geography is a film montage technique devised and developed by Russian cinematographer Lev Kuleshov in the 1920s (the 'Kuleshov effect' is a specific version of this technique). It is a type of editing in which shots from various places and times are combined to create a new, illusionary storyline set in one place and time. The montage relies on the viewer's natural urge to connect and make sense of combined sequences, despite the obvious illusion of the constructed linkages and montage (Levaco, 1974). An example could be a scene of somebody opening a door, followed by a still of a picturesque landscape. We would combine the two into a narrative of somebody stepping out of the door into that landscape, even though the two situations have different origins in reality.
In the context of contemporary urban landscapes, the concept of creative geography can help to reveal how spatial narratives are constructed. On urban development sites, for instance, we often find situated information materials, photos and maps telling us about the site's history and former functions. As French scholar and urban thinker Michel de Certeau points out, depicting a place by reference to the absence of something can be a way to create a spatial narrative (de Certeau, 1984/1988, p. 108) and establish a shared understanding of place. In addition, we find signs, maps or visuals illustrating the (more or less realistic) future of the site displayed at these locations too. As a visitor, you link these past, present and future ideas of the space – stories about heritage, your present embodied experience and the intended future visions blend together in an on-site version of creative geography.

Maria Gil Ulldemolins
Hasselt University
Faculty of Architecture & Arts
maria.gilulldemolins@uhasselt.be

Further readings

Allen, A. (1998). Power trouble: Performativity as critical theory. *Constellations, 5*(4), 456–471. https://doi.org/10.1111/1467-8675.00108

Rendell, J. (2010). *Site-writing: The architecture of art criticism.* I. B. Tauris.

Spry, T. (2006). A 'performative-I' copresence: Embodying the ethnographic turn in performance and the performative turn in ethnography. *Text and Performance Quarterly, 26*(4), 339–346. https://doi.org/10.1080/10462930600828790

Critical performativity

The concept of the 'performative' derives from language's ability to affect reality through statements known as 'utterances', as seen in the example of marriage vows (Allen, 1998, pp. 461–462). Following this, feminist philosopher Judith Butler points out that gender is performative, 'that is, constituting the identity it is purported to be' (quoted in Allen, 1998, pp. 459–460). Butler follows the philosopher Jacques Derrida's suggestion that a performative utterance depends on iteration, and hence on citation (Allen, 1998, p. 462): the marriage vows are recognised as valid because they are a repetition of an established ritual – they are cited. Accordingly, Butler proposes that 'a citation will be at once an interpretation of the norm and an occasion to expose the norm' (quoted in Allen, 1998, p. 462).

Inheriting these ideas, the concept of the *critical performative* refers to the possibility that critical engagements (i.e. analyses and interpretations of cultural works) are a form of identity enactment. This positioning allows critical theorists to conceive of their work as a practice with the possibility to challenge what has traditionally been perceived as a theoretical, objective and scientific study. Different fields have incorporated this approach. Ethnographers, for instance, have developed the notion of auto-ethnography, a form of study that does not shy away from the singular, embodied experiences of the researcher at work (what performance studies scholar Tami Spry (2006) suggests calling the 'performative-I'). In architecture, critic and historian Jane Rendell (2010) – cross-pollinating the discipline with art and writing – proposes 'site-writing'. Site-writing refuses the neutral interpreter. Instead, it reveals the autobiographical and embodied reality of the critic, and consequently raises questions about the power dynamics and politics of specific locations. Rendell also suggests that site-writing might develop a type of architectural writing in which the text is not simply *about* a site but can itself *become* a site. Even blending the fictional with the factual is possible without surrendering critical rigour.

Kris Pint
Hasselt University
Faculty of Architecture & Arts
kris.pint@uhasselt.be

Further readings
de Certeau, M. (1988). Spatial stories. In *The practice of everyday life* (pp. 115–130). University of California Press.

de Certeau, M. (1998). Ghosts in the city. In *The practice of everyday life, volume 2: Living and cooking* (pp. 133–144). University of Minnesota Press.

Delinquent narrative

Delinquent narrative is a concept that cultural critic Michel de Certeau uses to refer to stories, or fragments of stories, that cannot be recuperated for city branding or politics, or for the critical discourses of activists and researchers. These stories may express memories of the city, but they cannot be 'tamed' by a specific historical or nationalist framework.

The strange and haunting presence of these narratives, lingering in legends, practices, street names, ornaments and historic buildings, makes them heir to the ancient 'spirits of place'. Together, these stories form a mobile multitude that opens up another, mythical realm in ordinary urban life. They relate to the personal mythology of memories and unconscious associations explored by both psychoanalysis and surrealism. Examples of such narratives can be found in surrealist Louis Aragon's book *Le Paysan de Paris* (1926), director Federico Fellini's film *Roma* (1972), or more recently in documentaries such as director Gianfranco Rosi's *Sacro GRA* (2013). For de Certeau, these apparently insignificant, uncoded and unruly stories are necessary to sustain an inhabitable, 'believable' city.

Asma Mehan
University of Porto
Research Centre for Territory,
Transport and Environment (CITTA)
asmamehan@fe.up.pt

Further readings

Benjamin, W. (1999a). *The arcades project.* Harvard University Press.

Benjamin, W. (1999b). The destructive character. In M.W. Jennings, H. Eiland & G. Smith (Ed.), *Walter Benjamin: Selected writing, vol. 2.* (1931-1934). Cambridge: The Belknap Press of Harvard University Press. pp. 541-3.

Mehan, A. (2017). 'Tabula rasa' planning: Creative destruction and building a new urban identity. *Journal of Architecture and Urbanism, 41*(3), 210–220.

Tournikiotis, P. (1999). *The histography of modern architecture.* MIT Press.

Destructive character

In 1931, philosopher Walter Benjamin wrote a short piece titled 'The destructive character'. This text, one of Benjamin's *Denkbilder* ('thinking images') was written during one of the worst periods in German and European history: after the crisis of 1929, when European fascism was on the rise. Benjamin states:

The destructive character knows only one watchword: make room and only one activity: clearing away. It clears away the traces of our own age and has few needs, and the least of them is to know what will replace what has been destroyed. First, for a moment at least, empty space – the place where the thing stood or the victim lived. Someone is sure to be found who needs this space without occupying it. (Benjamin, 1999b, p. 541)

In a broader sense, the *destructive character* had equally been a feature of both the Renaissance and the Enlightenment, which presented themselves as new developments from the root. The concept also appeared in the works of the architect and writer Rem Koolhaas, where it set itself as a strategy of 'emptiness'. Koolhaas points to a number of different cities undergoing ambitious renovation plans and starting from a large urban void implemented for various reasons (Mehan, 2017).

Nevena Daković
University of Arts, Belgrade,
Film and Media Studies
n.m.dakovic@gmail.com

Further readings

Balázs, A., Apor, P., & Sándor, H. (Eds). (2018). The handbook of courage: Cultural opposition and its heritage in Eastern Europe. Research Centre for the Humanities, Hungarian Academy of Sciences.

De Boer, S. P., Driessen, E., & Verhaar, H. (1982). Biographical dictionary of dissidents in the Soviet Union: 1956–1975. Martinus Nijhoff.

Dissident heritage

Dissident heritage encompasses the culture and artistic heritage of dissidents, such as samizdat or *tamizdat* (i.e. self-publishing) practices in the Union of Soviet Socialist Republics (USSR) when censored and underground publications were manually reproduced and distributed. The dissidents appeared during the Cold War era as dissatisfied rebels, protestors, and ferocious critics of the communist regimes in the USSR and of socialist dictatorships in central, eastern and south-eastern Europe. Their emergence is associated with the realisation that traditional methods had no effect, when artists and intellectuals began to search for other non-violent forms of resistance, thereby creating a kind of 'revolution in revolution'. Hence the name 'dissident', which etymologically means 'sitting apart' from the regime. Today, the dissident as a marginalised intellectual or artist of the Cold War has become a central figure in the human rights imagination all over the world, and embodies local and global aspects. The latter are broadly associated with the issue of freedom of expression in post-socialist countries and the Third World, and with the collapse of bipolar Europe.

The values, meanings and importance of the worlds of dissident heritage spill over and imbue the history of cities, sites and buildings – turning the latter into site-specific artworks/installations, *lieux de mémoire* or *lieux de résistance* in the city (the shipyard in Gdansk, the National Theatre in Belgrade, places in Oran). Furthermore, dissident heritage is part of the broader phenomenon of the culture of dissent – people's ability to thoughtfully disagree. Dissident narratives can persuasively voice disagreements regarding a number of social or political issues that are further built into urban narratives. Recuperating a range of dissident heritage, urban narratives in turn can become chronicles of a dissident past and cultural opposition, the narrative and the dissident culture mutually affecting and enforcing each other.

Nevena Daković
University of Arts, Belgrade
Film and Media Studies
n.m.dakovic@gmail.com

Svava Riesto
University of Copenhagen
Landscape Architecture and Planning
svri@ign.ku.dk

Further readings

Ashworth, G., & Tunbridge, J. (1996). *Dissonant heritage: The management of the past as a resource in conflict.* Wiley.

Daković, N., Mijatović, L. R., & Nikolic, M. (2015). From dissonance to resilience: The heritage of Belgrade's Staro sajmiste. In E. Auclaire & G. Fairclough (Eds), *Theory and practice in heritage and sustainability: Between past and future* (pp. 190–203). Routledge.

Riesto, S., & Tietjen, A. (2018). Planning with heritage: A critical debate across landscape architecture practice and heritage theory. In E. Braae & H. Steiner (Eds), *Routledge companion to landscape architecture* (pp. 240–253). Routledge.

Smith, L. (2006). *Uses of heritage.* Routledge.

Dissonant heritage

'Dissonance' in music refers to a mingling of sounds that do not blend into one another harmoniously but create tension or even sound harsh. In discussions of urban heritage, 'dissonance' has been introduced to name the inevitable agonism and lack of consistency that is inherent to all heritage processes. Accordingly, the heritage of European cities is not harmonious and univocal, but is a contested domain of different, and often conflicting, versions of the past, present and future. Heritage scholars Turnbridge and Ashworth (1996, p. 22) emphasise the concepts of 'inheritance' and 'ownership' and state that all 'heritage is someone's heritage and therefore logically not someone else's'. Urban heritage can be claimed, appropriated, destroyed, used or excluded by different groups and individuals, leaving others disinherited. In this way, heritage has a 'particular power to legitimise or subvert someone's sense of place and identity' (Daković et al, 2015, p. 192; Smith, 2006, p. 82). Today, when many urban regions in Europe are using heritage as a resource in place-making, tourism and branding, there is a risk of 'editing out negative and conflicted heritage' in seemingly smooth and positive narratives that fit with (economic) development goals, without further discussion (Riesto & Tietjen, 2018, p. 249). It is thus important to be aware that all heritage is viewed differently by different urban groups and individuals. How can urban narratives be created on such dissonant terrain, and with what potential?

Willie Vogel
Delft University of Technology
Architecture
willie.c.vogel@gmail.com

Further readings

Dunn, N. (2016). *Dark matter: The sublime liquidity of the nocturnal city.* Zero Books.

Dunn, N., & Dubowitz, D. (2018). Dark inscriptions. *Writingplace, 2,* 81–97. https://doi.org/10.7480/writingplace.2.2641

Bikos, K., & Kher, A. (2020, March). Twilight, dawn, and dusk. *Time and Date.* https://www.timeanddate.com/astronomy/different-types-twilight.html

Tanizaki, J. (1977). *In praise of shadows.* Leete's Island Books.

Dusk

The world falls silent as the birds vigorously sing their last songs: it is *dusk*. In the northern sky, the Pole Star makes its appearance, a greeting from the night. In our practice of reading urban settings, time can be an interesting angle from which to look – especially in the periods of metamorphosis between day and night. Twilight moments are often described in poetry as having something magical about them. Clock time is then substituted with sunset, dusk or night, expressing an atmospheric stage rather than an exact moment. At dusk, the decorations on facades are often negated by the vibrations of the sun's rays hitting the surface. The angle of the sun reflects the light differently in the air's particles, creating new colours: 'In no other setting is gold quite so exquisitely beautiful', as the Japanese writer Junichiro Tanizaki puts it in his book *In praise of shadows* (Tanizaki, 1977, p. 22). Such moments, measured by sundials rather than clocks, give the urban setting a different kind of existence.

In urban settings, the moment of dusk is often invaded by lights and sounds from civilisation. Stars are outshone by 'constructed light' that pushes away the dark and frightening night. Are humans creating their own night-star language with high-rise towers that are always lit? What does this mean for the evolution of our eyes and our biological rhythms? Our rhythms between light and darkness are called the circadian clock – a 24-hour internal clock that is affected by environmental inputs such as light. Although the concept of the circadian clock is often used in genetics and biology, and has mainly been researched in plants and animals, humans are also affected by it. It might be that when we read the environment through the different stages of the day, rather than as divided into 24 hours, we experience this circadian clock.

Sara Santos Cruz
University of Porto
Research Centre for Territory,
Transport and Environment (CITTA)
scruz@fe.up.pt

Further readings

Baeten, G. (2001). Clichés of urban doom: The dystopian politics of metaphors for the unequal city – a view from Brussels. *International Journal of Urban and Regional Research, 25*(1), 55–69. https://doi.org/10.1111/1468-2427.00297

Cruz, S. (2004). *Fragmentos utópicos na cidade caótica: Condomínios fechados no Grande Porto* [Unpublished doctoral thesis, Universidade do Porto].

MacLeod, G., & Ward, K. (2002). Spaces of utopia and dystopia: Landscaping the contemporary city. *Geografiska Annaler: Series B, Human Geography, 84*(3–4), 153–170. http://www.jstor.org/stable/3554313

Merrifield, A. (2000). The dialectics of dystopia: Disorder and zero tolerance in the city. *International Journal of Urban and Regional Research, 42*(2), 473–489. https://doi.org/10.1111/1468-2427.00259

Dystopian narratives

Dystopia is a concept that dates from the 18th century and refers to an imperfect imagined place or society associated with great injustice and suffering. The word results from the combination of *dys*, meaning bad, with the Greek *topos* or place. As opposed to utopia – a perfect imagined place or society (*ou-topia* or non-place, merged with *eu-topia* or good place), dystopias describe unpleasant places and dehumanised societies. In literature, *dystopian narratives* present a nightmarish picture of the future. The main topics often refer to revolutions, wars, rebellions, injustices, poverty and disasters.

Urban landscapes result from a 'patchwork-quilt of urban spaces of utopia and dystopia' (MacLeod & Ward, 2002, p. 153) where idyllic landscapes – for example, secure protected enclaves (exclusive residential neighbourhoods, theme parks etc.) – easily emerge against outside spaces and threats associated with a hostile environment described as dystopian. By borrowing from dystopian literature, planners and urbanists can introduce an imaginative dimension into the representation of urban spaces and their problems, potentially enabling more significant transformations.

On the other hand, the complexity of the real world often presents more intricate challenges that are not suited to one-dimensional representations. Dystopian narratives vary as to whether (or not) they implicitly suggest an alternative, progressive future.

Dystopian narratives should enable creative urban interventions, rather than merely distorting the city with single narratives of the future and thereby limiting potentials and opportunities for change for the better (Cruz, 2004; Merrifield, 2000).

Angeliki Sioli
Delft University of Technology
Architecture
A.Sioli@tudelft.nl

Willie Vogel
Delft University of Technology
Architecture
willie.c.vogel@gmail.com

Further readings

Benjamin, W. (1999). *The arcades project.* Belknap Press.

Casey, S. E. (1998). *The fate of place: A philosophical history.* University of California Press.

Husserl, E. (1981). The world of the living present and the constitution of the surrounding world external to the organism. In P. McCormick & F. A. Elliston (Eds), *Husserl: Shorter works* (pp. 238–250). University of Notre Dame Press.

Solnit, R. (2001). *Wanderlust: A history of walking.* Granta.

Enactive walking

Foot by foot, step by step, one gradually attunes oneself to an urban landscape. The writer Rebecca Solnit author of *Wanderlust: A history of walking* (2001) explains that being on foot enables us to be in the world, navigating, changing perspective and getting through places. Although it is often an overlooked or taken-for-granted action of the able-bodied that conforms to the morphological topography of a city, walking is an actively embodied interaction with place. Philosopher Edward Casey reminds us that 'in walking we move into a near-sphere of our own choosing, if not of our making. In this sphere, we encounter places as much as we enliven them' (Casey, 1998, p. 229). Lived body and lived place link up with each other in the experience of walking, allowing us to 'build up a coherent world out of the fragmentary appearances of a city that, taken in isolated groupings, would be merely kaleidoscopic', as Edmund Husserl observes (Husserl, 1981, pp. 248–249). Thus, when we are trying to capture the city,
walking can be an excellent tool, an embodied way of knowing in which the action 'is both means and end, travel and destination' (Solnit, 2001, p. 6).

Unlike *flânerie, enactive walking* enables the active perception of an urban place. The 19th-century character of the *flâneur*, explored in depth by the philosopher Walter Benjamin in *The arcades project* (1999), maintains a clear distance from the city: he is an observer of the urban environment much more than he is a participant in it. The *flâneur* is interested in and intrigued by the phantasmagoria of the city, and the city remains at the level of retinal experience. Enactive walking is instead a consciously embodied interaction with the city, influencing and redefining the environment around it. With today's proliferation of mobile phones, walking apps, social media and constant developments in augmented reality, the experience of enactive walking can even redefine the environment in ways that were unimaginable in previous centuries.

Svava Riesto
University of Copenhagen
Landscape Architecture and Planning
svri@ign.ku.dk

Further readings

Rogoff, I. (2006). 'Smuggling': An embodied criticality. http://xenopraxis.net/readings/rogoff_smuggling.pdf

Rogoff, I. (2007). What is a theorist? In. J. Elkins & M. Newman (Eds.), *The State of Art Criticism.* (pp. 97-109). Routledge

Rogoff, I. (2005). Looking away: Participations in visual culture. In G. Butt (Ed.), *After criticism: New responses to art and performance* (pp. 117–134). Blackwell.

Tietjen, A., Riesto, S., & Haddad, R. (2017). Doing critique of what design does at Superkilen. *CRIOS: Critica degli ordinamenti spaziali,* 4(13), 45–60.

Embodied criticality

Criticality, as defined by art theorist and curator Irit Rogoff, is an embodied way of engaging with art, or with other cultural products such as (we might suggest here) designed urban spaces. Criticality positions itself differently from the established forms of art critique: criticism, the oldest practice, which is about judging a definable aesthetic object as 'good' or 'bad'; and critique, which is the post-structuralist examination of artworks, focusing on revealing their underlying assumptions, constitutive logics and power relations (Rogoff, 2005, p. 119; Rogoff, 2006, p. 1). Criticality, the most recent form of writing about art, emphasises the present and rejects the idea of immanent values (Rogoff, 2005). *Embodied criticality* seeks to 'inhabit a problem rather than analysing it' (Rogoff, 2006, p. 1). It is thus not a distant analysis, but seeks to actualise the potential (Rogoff, 2006) of, for example, a designed urban space. With criticality, one can question what an urban space *does* here and now, rather than judging it as good or bad or defining what it is (Tietjen et al., 2017). Criticality is a situated practice, and it involves risk and uncertainties. It can take many forms – for example writing, drawing and bodily performances (Tietjen et al., 2017).

Eliana Sousa Santos
CES Universidade de Coimbra
Architecture
esousasantos@ces.uc.pt

Further readings

Aelbrecht, P. S. (2016). Fourth places: The contemporary public settings for informal social interaction among strangers. *Journal of Urban Design, 21*(1), 124–152. https://doi.org/10.1080/13574809.2015.1106920

Oldenburg, R. (1997). *The great good place: Cafes, coffee shops, bookstores, bars, hair salons, and other hangouts at the heart of a community.* Marlowe. (Original work published 1989).

Fourth places

The concept of *fourth places* was coined by urban designer Patricia Simoes Aelbrecht (2016, p. 126) to analyse previously unnoticed informal social settings that occur on thresholds or in edge spaces in recently designed and developed urban areas.
Following the concept of 'third places' coined by urban sociologist Ray Oldenburg (1989/1997), Aelbrecht defines fourth places as a 'type of informal social space with similar social and behavioral characteristics, differentiation from work or home routines and inclusivity', but with 'mixed relational locales, more socially diverse in terms of user groups and social relations and realms, than "third places" that mainly cater for parochial life among socially homogeneous groups' (Aelbrecht, 2016, p. 134).
If third places are privately owned and partially public, fourth places are public and anonymous. According to Patricia Simoes Aelbrecht, some of these spaces are on the threshold between clearly public spaces, such as squares or streets, and private spaces such as shopping centres (Aelbrecht, 2016, p. 136). Aelbrecht mostly observed the thresholds, edges and paths in the large-scale planned neighbourhood of Parque das Nações in Lisbon, designed and built in the 1990s and 2000s. However, her definition of fourth places can be recognised in other types of area, such as formally designed or informally built urban clusters and recent or traditional developments.
'Fourth places' may be used conceptually as an additional category to define informal social settings, and it is important for discovering social narratives that change the occupation and perception of a public space through the collective actions of a community. In this way, the identification of fourth places that are specifically relevant to a determined community might develop subjective perceptions or mythologies – expanding them to fit major concepts such as urbanist Edward Soja's 'third space', itself derived from sociologist Henri Lefevbre's 'lived space' and philosopher Michel Foucault's 'other spaces'.

Henriette Steiner
University of Copenhagen,
Landscape Architecture and Planning
hst@ign.ku.dk

Kristin Veel
University of Copenhagen
Arts and Cultural Studies
kristinv@hum.ku.dk

Further readings

Heidegger, M. (1977). *The Age of the World Picture* (1938), in The Question Concerning Technology and Other Essays (New York: Harper Torchbooks, 1977), 115–154 – the quotation comes from page 135.

Steiner, H., & Veel, K. (2020). *Tower to Tower: Gigantism in architecture and digital culture.* MIT Press.

Gigantism

Gigantism describes material and immaterial structures that appear to be so big and all-encompassing that they have an overarching, ubiquitous quality to them, although they are never available to, or experienced in the same way by, everyone everywhere. For something to be identifiable as gigantism, however, there needs to be something more at work than simply a large scale. German philosopher Martin Heidegger notes this elusive quality:

[As] soon as the gigantic in planning and calculating and adjusting and making secure shifts over out of the quantitative and becomes a special quality, then what is gigantic, and what can seemingly always be calculated completely, becomes, precisely through this, incalculable.

In describing the gigantic as incalculable, Heidegger points to a shift or slide away from largeness in quantitative terms, towards the gigantic as a special quality that takes on a significance of its own and is therefore difficult, if not downright impossible, to measure. However, narratives can offer a way to grasp this special quality of the gigantic. As architectural scholars, we can start our investigation by climbing the gigantic structures we study – walking or taking an elevator to the top of the tallest built artefacts in our upward-expanding cities. As scholars of the digital fabric of the contemporary city, we can likewise take a ride outwards in gigantic digital networked structures, through the various interfaces we operate, to get a glimpse of their expansiveness as infrastructural systems dependent on digital structures of code. And as cultural researchers, we can trace, theorise and critically examine the trajectory of the emergence of these infrastructures, as well as their reflections in the images and narratives that pervade our cultural imagination – ranging from memes and viral YouTube clips to film, art, and literature.

This entry is based on material published in Steiner and Veel (2020).

Heidi Svenningsen Kajita
University of Copenhagen Landscape Architecture and Planning
hsk@ign.ku.dk

Further readings

Federici, S. (2018). *Witches, witch-hunting, and women.* Common Notions/Autonomedia/PM Press.

Tebbutt, M. (1995). *Women's talk? A social history of gossip in working class neighbourhoods, 1880–1960.* Scolar Press.

Gossip

Short-sighted histories and tales have again become apposite to Western communities. Reflexive practitioners and scholars employ ethnographic accounts, oral histories and other forms of evaluative language and analysis to question the consequences of socio-economic inequalities and the crisis of democracy for lived experiences. *Gossip* has surfaced in such nuanced descriptions. Feminist philosopher Silvia Federici turns to gossip to challenge the realm of rational discourse (Federici, 2018). Gossip is women's talk. And, contrary to the feminine ideal of silence, gossip is mostly associated with the non-ideal malicious nagging and tittle-tattle of idle women. But the word 'gossip' can be traced back to the Old English word *godsibb*, meaning relative to God. In the pre-modern era, gossip functioned as a means to maintain spiritual closeness and care for a child's well-being, and in more secular forms of caring for social relations such as neighbourliness. Following this positive trajectory, gossip defined (in the *Oxford English dictionary*) as 'easy, unrestrained talk or writing, especially about persons or social incidents' is known to play part in women's cooperation and the indirect reciprocity necessary to maintain social order (Tebbutt, 1995). Gossip reveals and shares the tight-knit and intimate ways of everyday life and community that otherwise remain inconspicuous. By circulating personal information, gossip threatens and disrupts the establishment. Gossip can entail a possibility to change the status quo.

In the context of urban narratives, gossip can be an instrument to make connections between communities' colloquial languages and experts' technical languages, which are mostly kept distinct. To access gossip requires a degree of membership, reciprocity and group solidarity. Such membership is not easily granted to outsiders. To get into the weaving of memories and the know-how of communities that gossip offers, experts therefore have to work *with* and not only *for* communities. Working with gossip can reveal what kind of work is needed.

Sara Santos Cruz
University of Porto
Research Centre for Territory, Transport and Environment (CITTA)
scruz@fe.up.pt

Further readings

Lourenço, E. (1986). Kierkegaard e Pessoa ou a s máscaras do absoluto. In *Fernando Rei da nossa Baviera* (pp. 97–109). Imprensa Nacional Casa da Moeda.

Madanipour, A. (2013). The identity of the city. In S. Serreli (Ed.), *City project and public space* (pp. 49–64). Springer.

McAdams, D. (2001). The psychology of life stories. *Review of General Psychology, 5*(2), 100–122. https://doi.org/10.1037/1089-2680.5.2.100

Ricoeur, P. (1991). Narrative identity. *Philosophy Today, 35*(1), 73–81.

Heteronym

In literary theory, a *heteronym* or alternative persona is a fictional personality that a writer creates (and shapes) in order to write as a number of distinct authors or personas, each one differing in style, philosophy and personality. The term was invented by the Portuguese poet Fernando Pessoa, who created nearly 80 such literary alter egos.
Heteronyms are different from pseudonyms, since the latter are 'false names' (from the Greek *pseudos* and *ónoma*). Philosopher Søren Kierkegaard's pseudonyms and Fernando Pessoa's heteronyms both involve the creation of imagined multiple personas, but Pessoa's heteronyms are placed at a higher level of depersonalisation, revealing the author's need for other individual identities (Lourenço, 1986).
Identity theorists consistently refer to the multiple identities of the individual. These multiple identities are distinct parts of one's self-concept, internal meanings and expectations related to one's social networks, different spatial contexts, and the roles each individual plays in relation to others.
Similarly to individuals, one can say that places and cities also have identities. Just as with individuals, and drawing on the notion of narrative identity (McAdams, 2001; Ricoeur, 1991), in cities we find not single narratives but multiple representations of places. Stories about a place are often diverse and even contradictory. Cities are made up of heterogeneous people and physical spaces. For Madanipour (2013, p. 58), 'one cannot rely on a single narrative and a rigid identity to describe all these differences. The result would inevitably be multiple and dynamic identities, changing over time and across space'. Thus, cities are living entities with a multiplicity of identities or heteronyms.

Sylvie Tram Nguyen
École Polytechnique Fédérale de Lausanne (EPFL)
Laboratory of Urbanism
sylvie.nguyen@epfl.ch

Further readings

Viganò, P., Arnsperger, C., Cogato Lanza, E., Barcelloni Corte, M., & Cavalieri, C. (2017). Rethinking urban form: Switzerland as a 'horizontal metropolis'. Urban Planning, 2(1), 88–99.

Viganò, P. (2018). The Horizontal Metropolis: A Radical Project. In *The Horizontal Metropolis Between Urbanism and Urbanization* (pp. 1-9). Springer, Cham.

Viganò, P., & Cavalieri, C. (Eds). (2019). The Horizontal Metropolis a Radical Project. Zurich Switzerland: Park Books.

Horizontal metropolis

The concept of the horizontal metropolis refers to current changes happening in cities and territories, whereby traditional centralised city models – characterised by a structured and hierarchical division between centre and periphery, urban and rural – have shifted and lost their formerly distinct characteristics. A diffused and hybrid territorial form is alleged to have taken shape in contemporary urbanisation, identified across the world through various concepts such as *città diffusa* in Italy, *banlieue radieuse* in Belgium, *Zwischenstadt* in Germany and *desakota* in Asia (Viganò et al., 2017, 2018).

Characterised by horizontality, with a self-organising system of communication, transport and economic activity, the horizontal metropolis valorises the emerging urban processes taking place within extended forms of urbanisation. The horizontal metropolis is envisioned as enhancing existing values related to spatial, natural and social capitals – for example, by upgrading different levels of infrastructure as they evolve within the territory.

In *The horizontal metropolis: A radical project* (Viganò and Cavalieri, 2019), new ideas are described for the future of diffused urbanised territories across the world. These include approaches to upgrading the city-territory via concepts shared with urban ecology, urban metabolism and territories of recycled production. Water, soil and energy are elementary to the production and reproduction of these city-territories, with the purpose of increasing spatial and social justice through equal accessibility and mobility across the landscape.

Mirza Emirhafizović
University of Sarajevo
Political Sciences
mirza.emirhafizovic@fpn.unsa.ba

Sonja Novak
Josip Juraj Strossmayer University of Osijek
Humanities
snovak@ffos.hr

Further readings

Bolt, Gideon. 2017. *Governing Urban Diversity: Creating Social Cohesion, Social Mobility and Economic Performance in Today's Hyper-diversified Cities.* Accessed 2020. www.urbandivercities.eu/about-divercities/.

Budnik, M., Grossmann, K., Haase, A., Haid, C., Hedke, C., Kullmann, K., & Wolff, M. (2017). *Divercities: Living with urban diversity – the case of Leipzig, Germany.* Faculty of Geosciences, Utrecht University.

European Policy Brief. (2013). *Hyper-diversity: A new perspective on urban diversity.* https://ec.europa.eu/research/social-sciences/pdf/policy_briefs/divercities_policy_brief_0913.pdf

Han, B.-C. (2005). *Hyperkulturalität: Kultur und Globalisierung.* Merve.

Hyper-diversity

In the last decades, cities have become increasingly diverse places, reflecting the heterogenous composition of their residents as a result of migration, class-related differences, and a spectrum of identities as well as preferred lifestyles, according to Divercities. In 2014, urban planning scholar Tuna Tasan-Kok and co-authors introduced the concept of *hyper-diversity* in order to describe 'an ever-growing complexity as well as a fluidity of social positions, senses of belonging, and identities' in cities (Budnik et al., 2017, p. 11). To measure diversity according to parameters such as ethnic or religious affiliation, socio-economic status, migration background, age, sex etc., however, only provides a limited view, since it mainly covers the measurable, quantitative aspects of this diversity, glossing over more qualitative issues concerning individuals' attitudes, behaviours, personal lifestyles, value orientations etc. These qualitative aspects might be understood by looking at how borders between different forms of culture gradually disappear, and how various cultural groups become interconnected as they merge and transform into what is often described as 'hyper-culturality'. Such processes have a temporal and a spatial dimension, and this leads to a new kind of proximity (Han, 2005), creating a great diversity of everyday cultural activities and forms of cultural expression, which is especially noticeable in large cities. Urban narratives can be a way to describe, interpret and discuss some of these qualitative elements of hyper-diversity and hyper-culturality in cities. In particular, stories from the 20th and 21st centuries, where globalisation affects cities significantly, reflect the contemporary, hyper-diverse urban situation.

Jana Čulek
Delft University of Technology
Architecture
J.Culek@tudelft.nl

Further readings

Eaton, R. (2001). *Ideal cities: Utopianism and the (un)built environment.* Thames & Hudson.

Choay, F. (1997). *The rule and the model: On the theory of architecture and urbanism.* MIT Press.

Howard, E. & Osborn, F.J. (1965) *Garden cities of tomorrow / by Sir Ebenezer Howard; Edited with a preface by F. J. Osborn, with introductory essay by Lewis Mumford,* Faber & Faber

Le Corbusier, P.E.J. (1930). *Ville radieuse.*

Ideal cities

Ideal cities are often seen as the architectural and urban counterpart to utopian literature. However, this is not always the case. Proposals for ideal cities, according to their etymology, contain both a perfected physical model of an ideal space (Latin *idea*, an intellectual conception or representation) and a corresponding notion that 'the physical form of a city [Latin *civitas*, a body of citizens who constitute a state] can both reflect and condition the workings of a society and the behaviour of its citizens' (Eaton, 2001, p.11). But although they contain both a projective physical model of an ideal space and a corresponding social and political ordering of its inhabitants, the modes of living that ideal cities propose are not always critical or innovative in relation to their historical contexts. Eaton (2001, p.12) therefore defines two main types of ideal city: reactive, 'where the city is "adjusted" to reflect an established social order' and strengthen the political ideals of the system in power; and proactive, where the city proposes a new type of social order and can therefore be considered utopian. While ideal cities such as those of the Renaissance would fall into the category of reactive ideal cities, most examples from the 19th and 20th centuries, such as Ebenezer Howard's *Garden cities of tomorrow* (1898) or Le Corbusier's *Ville radieuse* (1930), would be considered proactive and thus utopian. In a contemporary context, the notion of the ideal city becomes productive when its intention to produce better spaces is used as a creative catalyst for city planning. Although the implementation of an ideal city is inevitably unfulfillable, the creation of its vision is not, and as such it should be used as a productive method and driving force in design.

Kęstutis Zaleckis
Kaunas University of Technology
Urban Planning
kestutis.zaleckis@ktu.lt

Further readings

Hillier, B., Burdett, R., Peponis, J., & Penn, A. (1987). Creating life: Or, does architecture determine anything? *Architecture et Comportement/Architecture and Behaviour, 3*(3), 233–250.

Kim, Y. O. (2001). The role of spatial configuration. In John Peponis, Jean D. Wineman, Sonit Bafna (Ed.), *Spatial cognition: Proceedings of the 3rd International Space Syntax Symposium* (sec. 49.1–49.21). University of Michigan, College of Architecture & Urban Planning, 2001.

Peponis, J. (2012). Building layouts as cognitive data: Purview and purview interface. *Cognitive Critique, 6*, 11–52.

Zaleckis, K., Grazuleviciute-Vileniske, I., & Vitkuviene, J. (2018). Miestovaizdžio skaitomumas kaip tapatumo rodiklis. http://archmuziejus.lt/lt/miestovaizdzio-skaitomumas-kaip-tapatumo-rodiklis/

Intelligibility and readability

Space syntax looks at architectural spaces as networks, and calculates how a precise location depends on its position in a network. A spatial network is modelled as a mathematical graph using node centrality calculations. There are two types of centrality: global and local.

Intelligibility is calculated as a correlation between local and global syntactic features during axial analysis. According to Bill Hillier, 'a strong correlation, or "high intelligibility", implies that the whole can be perceived from the parts' (Hillier et al., 1987, p. 237). The intelligibility of public spaces might be seen as a quantitative way to analyse urban narratives generated in a city space based on dualities in it structure, e.g. intelligible versus unintelligible, demonstrated versus hidden, etc.

Despite its potential usefulness for the analysis of a cityscape-text, intelligibility has limitations, as it addresses features in the spatial structure and looks at public space on an axis, with no recognition of its width or other dimensions. By analogy with verbal texts, intelligibility could be seen as equivalent to legibility – the possibility to understand spatial urban configurations – in opposition to *readability* as the possibility to understand the social or cultural function of a space.

The readability of an urban spatial structure is addressed in the normalised model of the spatial-social readability of a cityscape (Zaleckis et all. 2018) based on the model of cognitive frame (Peponis, 2012). This model is based on the method of the visual graph analysis of space syntax, which allows us to investigate spatial configurations with greater precision. The normalised readability model was successfully tested by Zaleckis et al. (2018) in the analysis of more than 30 historic urban structures. It demonstrated the ability to identify the common genotypic features of cities belonging to the same cultural-spatial tradition – for example, medieval Islamic cities, medieval Western cities, Renaissance cities etc. At the same time, the model was sensitive enough to reflect individual peculiarities and differences, e.g. comparing modernist Soviet housing blocks in Lithuania with those in the rest of the former Soviet Union.

Marcel Pikhart
University of Hradec Králové
Applied Linguistics
marcel.pikhart@uhk.cz

Further readings

Hall, B., & Covarrubias, P. O. (2018). *Among cultures: The challenge of communication.* Routledge.

Jackson, J. (2014). *Introducing language and intercultural communication.* Routledge.

Interculturality

Cultural changes are under way in Europe in favour of globalisation and interculturality. These changes influence identities and urban narratives, and present a challenge to the ways communication is managed and represented in modern narratives. The grand narratives have recently been abandoned, and new practices are present around us; this is reflected in human interactions, and even in spatial layouts. Diversity based on binary oppositions and stereotypical approaches have recently been vastly abandoned by scholars and practitioners, and urban planning takes into account that studying interculturality and transferring it into urbanism is a must to combat bias and various forms of conflict and misunderstanding. The particular interpretive context of a given narrative must take interculturality into consideration in order to understand the rationale for diversity and difference. New narratives present in Europe must therefore be understood inasmuch they present a synergy of plurality when combined with traditional narratives.

Svava Riesto
University of Copenhagen
Landscape Architecture and Planning
svri@ign.ku.dk

Further readings

Possing, B. (2017). *Understanding biographies: On biographies in history and stories in biography*. University of Southern Denmark.

Kolen, J., Renes, H., & Hermans, R. (Eds). (2015). *Landscape biographies: Geographical, historical and archaeological perspectives on the production and transmission of landscapes*. Amsterdam University Press.

Riesto, S. (2017). *Biography of an industrial landscape: Carlsberg's urban spaces retold*. Amsterdam University Press.

Roymans, N., Gerritsen, F., Van der Heijden, C., Bosma, K., Kolen, J. Landscape Biography as Research Strategy. The Case of the South Netherlands Project. *Landscape Research* 34-3-, pp. 337-359.

Landscape biography

'Biography' comes from the Greek *bio graphein*, to write a life. As a literary genre, biographies are stories about and interpretations of a person's life (Possing, 2017). In landscape research, biography has been introduced a lens through which to investigate, interpret and engage with specific landscapes through their infinite 'life histories' (Kolen et al., 2015; Riesto, 2017). This perspective seems particularly relevant in the context of today's European cities, where an increasingly financially driven urban development is pushing for urban projects that leave little room for the diverse meanings, temporal depth and ecological entanglements of places.

In this context, a landscape biographical lens can be a way to discover the layered histories of urban places, including *longue durée* processes, and to understand the present moment as part of those temporalities. Biographical accounts of urban places do not need to impose a chronological order, but can mean engaging with sudden shifts, accumulated meanings, reorderings of the past, obduracies and recurrences. From this perspective, urban places can be understood at each point in time as the interim outcome the interplay between people's changing values, social practices, conflicts, and cultural imaginings with ecological dynamics, such as water, weather and soil, animals and plants (Kolen et al., 2015; Roymans et al., 2010, Riesto, 2017). Rather than thinking that places have 'a past' we can discover that the past is in plural, and be conscious of the interpretative, political and even future-oriented act of writing urban narratives. *Landscape biography* can critique authoritative narratives of place used in urban projects and contribute alternative narratives, nuances and polyphonies to open up the possibility of assembling other, more sustainable and inclusive futures for and with urban places.

Henriette Steiner
University of Copenhagen
Landscape Architecture and Planning
hst@ign.ku.dk

Kristin Veel
University of Copenhagen
Arts and Cultural Studies
kristinv@hum.ku.dk

Further readings

Gumbrecht, H. U. (2013). *After 1945: Latency as origin of the present.* Stanford University Press.

Gumbrecht, H. U., & Klinger, F. (2011). Latenz: *Blinde Passagiere in den Geisteswissenschaften.* Vandenhoeck & Ruprecht.

Steiner, H., & Veel, K. (2020). *Tower to Tower: Gigantism in architecture and digital culture.* MIT Press.

Latency

The term *latency* has a rich and diverse set of cultural-theoretical implications. Etymologically, 'latent' originally meant 'concealed' or 'secret'. It comes from the Latin *latentem* (nominative *latens*), the present participle of *latere* meaning 'to lie hidden, lurk, be concealed', which is also related to the Greek *lethe* ('forgetfulness, oblivion') and *lethargos* ('forgetful'). Cultural theorist Hans Ulrich Gumbrecht has used the term 'latency' to argue that the 20th-century Western conception of time has been transformed: whereas a linear directionality that aimed towards change and progress was once dominant, now a condition of simultaneity that he calls a 'broad present' – a present where it is impossible for us to leave the past behind – has taken over. He links this transformation to the period after the Second World War, and he analyses it from the perspective of Germany, where the communist East and capitalist West both tried to leave the past behind and move on, economically as well as morally. Although both states touted narratives of progress towards a brighter future and a break with the past, there was nevertheless something that was impossible to leave behind. That 'something' can rear its head in narratives and representations of the city, whether in fiction and other media or in the narratives we hear and tell about our temporal experience of cities and urban life. For example, in director Wong Kar-wei's film *In the mood for love* (2000), the story of a slow, largely unresolved and secretive love affair is told in a filmic language of suspense, using techniques where the activities of some protagonists literally take place at a different speed from the rest of the scene.

This entry is based on material published in Steiner and Veel (2020).

Sonja Novak
Josip Juraj Strossmayer University of Osijek
Humanities
snovak@ffos.hr

Further readings

Halbwachs, M. (1950). *La mémoire collective.* Presses Universitaires de France.

Le Rider, J., Csáky, M., & Sommer, M. (2002). *Transnationale Gedächtnisorte in Zentraleuropa (Gedächtnis, Erinnerung, Identität 1).* Studien-Verlag.

Nora, P. (1997). *The realms of memory: Rethinking the French past.* Columbia University Press.

Lieux de mémoire

The concept of memory sites or *lieux de mémoire* comes from the French historian Pierre Nora, and it describes the idea that both individual and cultural memories can arise from certain places, objects or events which bear symbolic meaning for the local, regional or national community. Memory sites are places, events or objects representing points for the collection of memories that help to define individual and collective identities. Nora distinguishes between material memory spaces (e.g. regions, cities or buildings, which can function on multiple scales) and immaterial memory spaces such as dates, historical personages, institutions, works of art etc. Even though he differentiates between these material and immaterial phenomena, he still calls both of them 'sites', which in some way implies a form of material place, or at least a mental space. Noteworthy examples of memory sites are cities in e.g. central Europe that are characterised by multiple cultural codes, such as Breslau/Wrocław and Pressburg/Bratislava/Pozsony. These can be viewed as cities with split spaces of memory with both national and regional significance because of the multitude of ethnic groups that have inhabited them.
The multiple function of such memory sites arises from the fact that memories are not always univocal and unifying; moreover, there are also multiple layers of different splits, thus creating a complex set of symbols that are individually specific to different times (e.g. what is a memory for one generation may be forgotten or reinterpreted by the next), sociopolitical contexts (e.g. various political regimes) or different ethnicities (e.g. there may be contestations within ethnic groups as well). Moreover, there may be some places – e.g. *Denkmäler* – that are official sites of memory, while there may also be memory sites that are less authoritative and official, and that are very personal and intimate. In the context of writing urban narratives, it could be argued that each (especially canonical) text thematising a city – e.g. in the form of a historical novel or *Zeitroman* – is a sort of memory site that can have an effect in terms of changing perceptions or raising awareness of both individual and collective identities.

Matej Nikšič
Urban Planning Institute of the Republic of Slovenia
Architecture and Urbanism
matej.niksic@uirs.si

Further readings

Nikšič, M., Goršič, N., Tominc, B., Selloni, D., Galluzzo, L., Fassi, D., Peyricot, O., & Daeron, I. (2018). *Human cities: Challenging the city scale – investigation.* Cite du Design. http://www.uirs.si/pub/01_human_cities_challenging_the_city_scale_2014-2018_investigation.pdf

Schorr, L. B., & Schorr, D. (1988). *Within our reach: Breaking the cycle of disadvantage.* Anchor Press/Doubleday.

Local hero

A *local hero* is a citizens' representative, an active member of the local community, who with her/his knowledge, abilities, spare time etc. contributes to changes in the physical and/or social fabric of the local environment to make it a better place for living, working and socialising. The local hero can be a protagonist in stories of urban regeneration. In some cases, this character emerges from a deprived urban area that is in need of comprehensive urban regeneration and is not part of official regeneration programmes or schemes. The local hero is an agent of change who generates new local narratives, encouraging others to follow his/her example. A local hero acts in a bottom-up manner and is (at least initially) not part of any official structures. According to the Human Cities network, local heroes very often invest their time and energy in developing broader local civil initiatives, with a high level of motivation and emotional involvement (Nikšič et al., 2018). As Schorr and Schorr (1988) point out, individuals with the characteristics of local heroes are often social innovators too, as they help to find new ways of improving communities through locally tailored approaches where official institutional agendas may fail.

Juan A. García-Esparza
Universitat Jaume I
Architectural Conservation
juan.garcia@uji.es

Further readings

DeSilvey, C. (2017). *Curated decay: Heritage beyond saving.* Minnesota University Press.

García-Esparza, J. A. (2019). Beyond the intangible-tangible binary in cultural heritage: An analysis from rural areas in Valencia region, Spain. *International Journal of Intangible Heritage*, 14 (1), 123–137.

García-Esparza, J.A., & Altaba, P. (2018). Time, cognition and approach. Sustainable strategies for abandoned vernacular landscapes. *Sustainability* 10 (8): 2712-33.

Manicure(d)

If you *manicure* something, you care for it by softening, cutting and polishing some elements. This involves care and treatment to make something look better according to some set of aesthetic principles. Something that is manicured, such as a garden, is well cared for and looks very tidy. In terms of the built environment, the fact of manicuring a place might prevent things happening by happenstance. Happenstance is when something happens because of certain circumstances, without being planned by anyone. A historic environment can be created or transformed by happenstance if its social value is left to evolve and coexist with its historic and architectonic values. In critical heritage studies, a manicured place can be linked to the rejection of the unscripted: caring too much about a place might weaken one's desire to know what will happen next, and in turn might overlook the vibrant possibilities of the unexpected.

In this regard, cultural heritage is highly affected by dynamism. This dynamism emphasises scalar uncertainty in enhancing contemporary cultural processes in manicured cities. The understanding of place is thus a complex grammar that is only explained by heterodox approaches to cultural heritage where the manicured leaves room for recreation and forgetting.

Lamila Simisic Pasic
International University of Sarajevo
Philosophy & Architecture
lmsimisic@gmail.com

Further readings

Dawkins, R. (1989). *The selfish gene.* Oxford University Press.

Deleuze, G. (1993). *The fold: Leibniz and the baroque.* Athlone Press

Leibniz, G. W. (1898). *The monadology.* Clarendon Press. Memes

Memes

The term *memes* refers to products of culture that have evolved throughout history: living structures, or units of cultural transmission, which widen the concept of evolution. According to the biologist Richard Dawkins, memes include:

Tunes, ideas, catch-phrases, clothes fashions, ways of making pots or of building arches. Just as genes propagate themselves in the gene pool by leaping from body to body via sperms or eggs, so memes propagate themselves in the meme pool by leaping from brain to brain via a process which, in the broad sense, can be called imitation. (Dawkins, 1989, p. 192)

Today's digital platforms, especially Web 2.0, provide anyone with the possibility to make a meme.
Correlated with 'memes', the term 'monads', first presented by the 17th/18th-century philosopher Leibniz are seen as entities that are compounds without any parts. A monad, according to Leibniz, is a single substance as 'elements of things' without possibilities for extension and form (Leibniz, 1898).
By contrast with these closed entities, the 20th-century philosopher Deleuze's 'nomads' are elements that have been 'exposed' to dramatic transformations. Nomads transform via 'operable windows' that make their boundaries foldable (Deleuze, 1993). Such permeable boundaries of form are not only related to spatial performance, but also allow transformations on cultural, political and aesthetic levels.
Today, amid an abundance of informative, transmissive, sensible, responding, reflecting, resonating, adaptable or changeable boundaries, where practices of copying and pasting form new media-technological environments, monads, nomads and memes can be seen in a new light. They may provide new insights for analyses of and communications about the spatial and mental boundaries of urban places.

Saskia de Wit
Delft University of Technology
Landscape architecture
S.I.deWit@tudelft.nl

Further readings

Lerup, L. (2000). *After the city.* MIT Press.

Sieverts, T. (1997). *Zwischenstadt: Zwischen Ort und Welt, Raum und Zeit, Stadt und Land.* Birkhäuser.

Steenbergen, C., & Reh, W. (2011). *Metropolitan landscape architecture.* Birkhäuser.

Metropolitan landscape

Mid-size cities can be understood as components of their larger framework: a hybrid and complex *metropolitan landscape* which is a profound mix of city and landscape, nature and culture, spaces and flows. This urban-landscape system is characterised by multiple modes of organisation and dynamic socio-spatial processes. The metropolitan landscape is the landscape of the Anthropocene: not so much a new landscape type, but a new way of looking that replaces the classical urban-rural dichotomy with a range of all kinds of urbanity, landscape and infrastructure. These are not clearly divided but exist on a gradient, including diffusion (horizontal metropolis) as well as densification (vertical metropolis), where even the most urban area is influenced by the landscape underneath, and the most natural area is influenced by urban forces. Historically, urban and rural realms were divided administratively, economically and in planning terms. But these notions, based on clear distinctions between core city and urban fringe, centre and periphery, city and landscape, town and country, are not able to address the current condition of a polycentric, fragmented and patchwork urban-landscape fabric. According to architect Lars Lerup (2000), in this unstable, dynamic environment the continuity and compositional logic of the classical city appears to have been replaced with a contiguity of elements and networks, different spatial conditions that exist next to and on top of each other, in a constant process of formation.
Landscape architects Clemens Steenbergen and Wouter Reh (2011) defined the metropolitan landscape as a hybrid of two systems. One is that of nature and the agricultural landscape. This is set over against the spatial system of the city. Each has its own topography, spatial form and visual structure, and their structure and morphology overlap and interact rather than merely lying next to each other. The landscape interacts with the urban condition as a permanent, underlying substructure, as a physical open space system, and as a metabolic process. This interaction leads to various intermediate spatial forms characterised by flexible and dynamic relationships, congestion, layering and interpenetration.

Ida Sandström
Lund University
Architecture and Built Environment
ida.sandstrom@arkitektur.lth.se

Further readings

Deleuze, G., & Guattari, F. (1986). *Kafka: Toward a minor literature*. University of Minnesota Press.

Katz, C. (1996). Towards minor theory. *Environment and Planning D: Society and Space*, 14(4), 487–499.

Sandström, I. (2019). *Towards a Minor Urbanism: Thinking Community without Unity in Recent Makings of Public Space* . lund: Department of Architecture and Built Environment, Lund University.

Minor urbanism

The notion of *minor urbanism* arises from an interest in critical suggestive approaches to urban design. It stays particularly attentive to practices that are located outside of habitual or established modes of urbanism but inside the institutions of urban planning. This outside-inside position is the critical potential of minor urbanism: it does not act in opposition to institutional frameworks, but performs a criticality from within (Sandström, 2019).

The suggestive promise of minor urbanism is further exposed if one breaks down the term. The first word, 'minor', represents an elastic, critical force that acts in the cracks in major practices or institutions and affects them from within. The second word, 'urbanism', is here used for the professional production of a city. Minor urbanism is thus the professional production of a city that affects the major practices of urban planning from within the institutions. The minor introduces variations into the major by performing suggestive resistance from within. Consequently, a minor urbanism can become a counterpart to mainstream urban productions, but it can never happen outside or independently of them. This – the possibility of setting up a minor practice from within the major – is the revolutionary quality that has previously been discussed in relation to literature (Deleuze & Guattari, 1986) and theory (Katz, 1996).

Although most practices of minor urbanism share an interest in temporary and unstable conditions, as well as situated and collective ways of working, the minor cannot be characterised as one particular set of practices. It must on the contrary always be understood in relation to the major practices in which it resides. If the major is what supports and stabilises systematic ways of doing things, the minor is what may resist and rework the social relations of such dominant practices, as seen in a number of recent makings of public space (Sandström, 2019).

Karen Lens
Hasselt University
Faculty of Architecture & Arts
karen.lens@uhasselt.be

Further readings

Duburg, A., & van der Tol, R. (2008). *Moulage: Kunst en Vakmanschap in Modevormgeving*. Uitgeverij d'jonge Hond.

Lens, K. (2017). The ritual aspect of time in (religious) heritage: Balance between daily and sacred life as a link between past and future. In Fiorani, D., Kealy, L., Musso, S., Houbart, C., Plevoets, B. (managing ed.), & Van Cleempoel, K. (Eds.). *Conservation – adaptation – keeping alive the spirit of the place – adaptive reuse of heritage with symbolic value* (pp. 163–172). EAAE.

Lens, K. (2020). *Adaptive reuse of monastic heritage: Cloth maker's moulage as alternative thread to an architectural master plan* [Unpublished doctoral thesis, University of Hasselt].

Lens, K., & Van Cleempoel, K. (2019). Monasteries: The layered capture of rhythm in space and time through rituals by 'moulage'. *Interiors, 6*(3), 289–305.

Moulage

Moulage is a concept originating from the fashion and tailoring scene. It is a combination of *coupe* (pattern-making) and draping fabrics. This method is commonly employed in haute couture because of its degree of detail, intensity and need of time. When implemented during the complex adaptive reuse of architectural and landscape heritage, it facilitates a researcher, heritage consultant and/or designer to develop a new programme without reaching deadlock with a rigorous master plan. It helps to communicate about still-present original pattern pieces and how they are interwoven in the movable or draped context. It identifies which specific interventions are essential to launch the adaptive reuse in peaceful consultation with all stakeholders. On an urban level, moulage can also be an alternative to spartan master planning and to deal with the unexpected in both the short and long run. Looking for a small but realistic moulage node is a respectful way to buy time in complex transformation processes or to develop new rituals to pursue sustainable ownership.

Sara Santos Cruz
University of Porto
Research Centre for Territory,
Transport and Environment (CITTA)
scruz@fe.up.pt

Further readings

Engels, A., & Walz, K. (2018). Dealing with Multiperspectivity in real-world laboratories: Experiences from the transdisciplinary research project Urban Transformation Laboratories. *GAIA Ecological Perspectives for Science and Society, 27*(1), 39–45. https://doi.org/10.14512/gaia.27.S1.10

Hartner, M. (2012). *Multiperspectivity: The living handbook of narratology.* Interdisciplinary Centre for Narratology, University of Hamburg. https://www.lhn.uni-hamburg.de/node/37.html

Multiperspectivity

Multiperspectivity or 'polyperspectivity' is a way of narrating or representing that refers to multiple perspectives or points of view. It can be either 'a basic aspect of narration or a mode of storytelling in which multiple and often discrepant viewpoints are employed for the presentation and evaluation of a story and its storyworld' (Hartner, 2012). Examples of Multiperspectivity can be traced back to the 13th century *Edda*, or even to Plato's *Symposium*, but its use expanded in the 18th and 19th centuries with the discovery of point of view.

However, the concept cannot be narrowly applied to situations where there are several viewpoints, because this situation is found in most stories. Therefore, the usage of the concept 'has to be restricted to cases where points of view interact in salient and significant ways and thus create multiperspectivity by, for instance, repeatedly portraying the same event from various different angles' (Hartner, 2012).

The application of the concept to the urban context is undoubtedly crucial and valuable, and can be done in quite different situations. Urban analysis is usually characterised by multiple different perspectives rather than a homogeneous, consensual and shared vision of a common goal. To think about urban spaces is to think about different actors, agents, societal groups etc. with diverse needs and concerns. For example, in collaborative approaches, incorporating all the different perspectives instead of 'forcing all partners to accept a unified perspective' may be the key to a fruitful and genuine collaboration (Engels & Walz, 2018, p. 39).

Matthew Skjonsberg
ETH Zürich
Regional Design and Landscape Architecture
skjonsberg@arch.ethz.ch

Further readings

Armitage, K. C. (2009). *The nature study movement: The forgotten popularizer of America's conservation ethic.* University Press of Kansas.

Bailey, L. H. (1903). *The nature-study idea: Being an interpretation of the new school-movement to put the child in sympathy with nature.* Doubleday.

Comstock, A. B. (1911). *The handbook of nature study.* Cornell University Press.
Geddes, P. (1923). *Life: Outlines of general biology.* Harper & Bros.

Kohlstedt, S. G. (2010). *Teaching children science: Hands-on nature study in North America, 1890–1930.* University of Chicago Press.

Skjonsberg, M. (2018). Nature pattern. In *A new look at civic design: Park systems in America* (pp. 407–420) [Thesis 8095, EPFL].

Nature study

Finding historical precedents in the popularisation of amateur scientific practices on one hand, and in rural community practices on the other, *nature study* is both a concept and a method that is particularly relevant for our era. It shows how ecological armatures linking rural and urban settlements provide an effective setting for the first-hand observation of nature. This ecological accessibility, whereby ecological continuity enables active mobility (walking, cycling etc.), is particularly well suited to reading, writing and lifelong learning. From wetlands and riverfronts to community gardens, nature study has informed community values, contributing to the sympathetic integration of ecological habitats relating to the urban, the rural and the wilderness (Skjonsberg, 2018).
The pedagogical practice of nature study – teaching science through the direct observation of nature – was explicitly advocated by such self-described 'ruralists' as Frederick Law Olmsted, Patrick Geddes and Frank Lloyd Wright as well as biologists Liberty Hyde Bailey and Anna Botsford Comstock, and rural sociologists Evelyn Dewey, John Dewey and William James. For Frank Lloyd Wright, nature study was the central architectural concept – the geometric 'nature pattern' underlying each of his architectural designs was derived from it – and Patrick Geddes used the term interchangeably with 'ecology', prompting him to write: 'Anyone who deals with animate nature cannot get past the fact of beauty – it is as real in its own way as the force of gravity' (1923, p. 38).
The nature study idea was extensively developed at Cornell University in the early 1900s (Bailey, 1903; Comstock, 1911), and it provided the basis for nature study programmes in state schools across America, and for 'America's conservation ethic' (Armitage, 2009; Kohlstedt, 2010). Nature study has had many literary trajectories, including popular environmentalist texts such as Aldo Leopold's *A Sand County almanac* (1949) and Rachel Carson's *Silent spring* (1962), and the pedagogical traditions of Jean-Jacques Rousseau, Johann Heinrich Pestalozzi and Rudolf Steiner – for each of whom the practice of nature study was a central tenet. On the conceptual side, 'nature study for design' began with the first-hand observation of natural phenomena as interpreted through abstraction and analogy, anticipating such contemporary concepts and methods as biomimicry.

Matthew Skjonsberg
ETH Zürich
Regional Design and
Landscape Architecture
matthew.skjonsberg@epfl.ch

Saskia de Wit
Delft University of Technology
Landscape architecture
S.I.deWit@tudelft.nl

Further readings

Clément, G. (2008). *Planetary gardens: The landscape architecture of Gilles Clément*. Birkhäuser.

Desimini, J. (2013). Notions of nature. In M. Mariani & P. Barron (Eds), *Terrain vague: Interstices at the edge of the pale* (pp. 173–186). Routledge.

Geuze, A., & Skjonsberg, M. (2010). Second nature: New territories for the exiled. In Y. Hung & G. Aquino (Eds), *Landscape infrastructure* (pp. 24–29). Birkhäuser.

Hofmeister, S. (2009). Natures running wild: A social-ecological perspective on wilderness. *Nature and Culture, 43*(3), 293–315.

New natures

In 45 BCE the Roman writer Cicero conceived of a differentiation between 'first' and 'second' nature. First nature was the wilderness, the realm of the gods, untouched by human hands. It was also the raw material for second nature: the landscapes resulting from the cultivation of soil, the building of houses and the mining of minerals. Rural and urban were seen as mutually interrelated counterparts of the same civilising force. This thinking stands at the heart of a wide range of concepts that developed around the turn of this century, seeking to define a new theoretical framework for the relation between city and nature. Concepts such as 'second nature' (landscape architect Adriaan Geuze), 'third wilderness' (cultural ecologist Sabine Hofmeister), 'third landscape' (landscape architect Gilles Clément), 'fourth nature' (ecologist Ingo Kowarik, Jill Desimini) and 'new nature' (landscape architect Cristophe Girot) attempt to grasp a new type of nature: a hybrid between forms of urbanisation and ecological systems. They range from intentional designed ecologies as strategies for urbanisation processes to spontaneous ecologies as results of urban processes.
On one end of the spectrum stands the resuscitation of the term 'second nature' by Geuze and Skjonsberg (2010) as a regional strategy in advance of the city, combining Cicero's definition with the connotations of behavioural second nature – our learned, socialised human nature. The built environment normalises our behavioural second nature. One might say, for instance, that in a society that actively recycles, the act of recycling becomes second nature. But without the infrastructure to support recycling, that learned behaviour is quickly unlearned. Here, 'second nature' specifically describes a designed ecology created adjacent to existing human settlements, as an ecological armature capable of absorbing the growth of future settlements while systematically maintaining ecological continuity. On the other end is the notion of 'third landscape' (Clément, 2008), which is connected to specific types of urbanity: leftover or abandoned spaces. The colonisation of such spaces by natural processes results in an unwieldy and complex ruderal ecology, resulting from neglect and decay, but also an opportunity for spontaneous revival, the birth of a new cooperation of nature and culture. This 'new nature' has in common with 'first' nature that it is self-reproductive and exists in cycles, rather than in linear time heading towards a human goal.

Saskia de Wit
Delft University of Technology
Landscape architecture
S.I.deWit@tudelft.nl

Further readings

Bacon, E. (1974). *Design of cities*. Viking Press.

de Wit, S. I. (2018). *Hidden landscapes: The metropolitan garden as a multi-sensory expression of place*. Architectura & Natura Press.

Potteiger, M., & Purinton, J. (1998). *Landscape narratives: Design practices for telling stories*. Wiley.

Tuan, Y. (1977). *Space and place: The perspective of experience*. University of Minnesota Press.

Paths

As opposed to the abstract bird's-eye perspective of top-down urban planning, from the 1970s onwards urban planners such as Edmund Bacon (1974) approached the analysis and design of urban landscapes from the narrative, spatio-temporal perspective of the experiencing subject moving through the city. Such a spatiotemporal continuity is like an inverted narrative: where literary narrative unfolds in time and the space of action is suggested, in the space of the physical city the dimension of time is suggested by *paths*.
The narrative structure of such a sequence may be a simple chain of events with a beginning, middle and end, be embellished with diversions, digressions and picaresque twists, be accompanied by subplots, or fork into blind alleys like the alternative scenarios explored in a detective novel. The elaboration of the plot is provided by the physical structure: the theatrical staging of spaces, the steepness of slopes or stairs, changes in direction, entrances, landmarks, vistas etc. These structural elements are not so much images with defined meanings as they are perceivable bodily kinaesthetic events that allow each and every visitor to create their own meaning, with the path as a shared storyline.
The relationship between space and time directly appeals to bodily experience. The human body is able to consider space and time (distance and tempo) because they are felt as a biological arc of effort and rest, tension and relaxation. Thus, space, time and bodily experience coexist, interlocking and defining each other on a route, as an expression of the urban composition.

Ann Petermans
Hasselt University
Faculty of Architecture & Arts
ann.petermans@uhasselt.be

Marcel Pikhart
University of Hradec Králové
Applied Linguistics
marcel.pikhart@uhk.cz

Further readings

Altman & Low (1992). *Place Attachment: Human Behavior and Environment vol. 12.* New York: Plenum Press.

Hayden, D. (1995). *The power of place: Urban landscapes as public history.* MIT Press.

Jack, G. (2012). The role of place attachments in wellbeing. In S. Atkinson, S. Fuller & J. Painter (Eds), *Wellbeing and place* (pp. 89–103). Ashgate.

Manzo, L., & Devine-Wright, P. (Eds). (2014). *Place attachment: Advances in theory, methods and applications.* Routledge.

Scannell, L., & Gifford, R. (2010). Defining place attachment: A tripartite organizing framework. *Journal of Environmental Psychology, 30*, 1–10.

Place attachment

Place attachment relates to the affective bonds that exist between people and the environments that are significant to them (Low & Altman, 1992). It is bound up with human experiences, a sense of meaning, social connectedness and belongingness. It evolves out of regular person-environment interactions and the meanings associated with them, and thus has its origins in childhood (Jack, 2012). The concept can be used to explore how and why people feel attached to particular places, and where this attachment originates. As a consequence, the phenomenology of space and place in urban narratives provides an important source for urban planning, because it can only be managed properly if understood from the perspective of the importance of place for individuals and communities. Place presents a crucial aspect of our lives because it creates our identities, gives meaning to our lives, and can improve societal processes and actions. Sentimental and emotional rootedness, belonging and bonding are very important for mobility and immigration, but also for urban planning, housing development and the management of urban infrastructures. In connection with intercultural societies and new narratives of European cities based on globalisation, place attachment is a source of identity, and understanding it is crucial for all place-making professions, and for the exploration of a diverse range of places and spaces and their meanings for very diverse groups of people. Place attachment can, however, also be approached through a more critical lens, implying that there is a power aspect connected to it (Hayden, 1995).

Ann-Charlott Eriksen
University of Copenhagen
Landscape Architecture and Planning
anncharlotteriksen@gmail.com

Further readings

Eriksen, A. (2019). *Into the green facades: Values ascribed to a popular cultural phenomenon in contemporary urban development* [Unpublished doctoral thesis, University of Copenhagen]. https://issuu.com/anncharlotteriksen/docs/into_the_green_facades_phd_thesis_anncharlott_erik

Myers, N. (2015). Edenic apocalypse: Singapore's end-of-time botanical tourism. In H. Davis & E. Turpin (Eds), *Art in the Anthropocene: Encounters among aesthetics, politics, environments and epistemologies* (pp. 31–42). Open Humanities Press.

Myers, N. (2017). From the Anthropocene to the Planthropocene: Designing gardens for plant/people involution. *History of Anthropology, 3*(28), 297–301.

Planthropocene

While urban narratives are often based on a silent hierarchy that puts people first, the concept of the *Planthropocene* offers a potentially new lens to study urban places. The term was introduced by anthropologist Natasha Myers as a critique of the Anthropocene, insisting that 'we are only because they [the plants] are' (Myers, 2017, p. 297). Myers argues that since all cultures, both local and global, revolve around plants, 'photosynthesis' should be a keyword for the present era (Myers, 2015) – and thus, we may add, should play a more important role in urban narratives.
Plants in this context are not separate from humans but cohabit in various environments and contexts in European cities. Nevertheless, people's relationships with plants are always defined by certain power nexuses, which often remain unspoken yet are profoundly inter-implicated (Myers, 2015, 2017). Myers calls for a more nuanced and critical approach towards the ways in which 'people stage relations with plants – whether these relations are intimate, extractive, violent, or instrumentalizing' (Myers, 2017, p. 297). The concept carries a wish for increased thoughtfulness about the effects of design and planning actions, and the narratives and values that they rely upon. 'Planthropocene' directs attention to the lives and actions of plants, thinking about plants as forces shaped by and shaping humans and the physical environment, and about how potential synergies can be created between plants and people.
As a lens through which to read and write urban places, 'Planthropocene' can stimulate the description of relationships between plants and people in specific urban situations: for example, how people and plant interrelate in acts of design and maintenance (or the lack thereof), in representations of urban places in architectural drawings, plans and photographs, or in everyday life in the city.

Willie Vogel
Delft University of Technology
Architecture
willie.c.vogel@gmail.com

Further readings

Butler, S. (1878). *Life and habit.* Jonathan Cape.

Carlisle, C. (2014). *On habit: Thinking in action.* Routledge.

Malabou, C. (2008). *What should we do with our brain?* Fordham University Press.

Malabou, C., Alliot, J., & Street, A. (2017). Thresholds of resistance: Between plasticity and flexibility. In A. Street, J. Alliot & M. Pauker (Eds), *Inter views in performance philosophy* (pp. 161–168). Palgrave Macmillan.

Plasticity

Plasticity comes from the Greek *plassein*, 'to mould', and it refers to the capacity to both receive form and give form (Malabou, 2008, p. 5). The concept of plasticity might be relevant for understanding the formation of and changes within a person, society or environment. The philosopher Catherine Malabou investigates how we mould our own brains in relation to our habits. According to her, plasticity is the ability to offer some resistance but simultaneously give way to change:

The brain is not merely a computer-like system which reflects, rather, it is the neural activity of our systems, it is a working. Plasticity is situated in between two extremes: the sensibility of taking a certain form and the demolition of a form. (Malabou, 2008, p. 5)

The philosopher Clare Carlisle also uses the term 'plasticity' and relates it to the term 'flexibility', which for her is the ability to immediately react to change without much resistance (Carlisle, 2014, p. 21). Plasticity seems to be the more advisable of the two, as it is less fluid, will not bend immediately, but at the same time will not allow habit to persist when change is needed. Plasticity is a coming together of resistance and receptivity, between contemplation and contraction. Between fixed habits, there is space to deviate. These moments of deviation are moments of contemplation, and are junctions where one consciously interacts with the environment. In urban research and design, the notion of plasticity can help us to understand that cities and inhabitants are not mere marionettes: they react to change, and thus are moulded and moulding.

Asma Mehan
University of Porto
Research Centre for Territory, Transport and Environment (CITTA)
asmamehan@fe.up.pt

Further readings

Kozlowski, M., Mehan, A., & Nawratek, K. (2020). *Kuala Lumpur: Community, infrastructure and urban inclusivity*. Routledge.

Nawratek, K. (2011). *City as a political idea*. University of Plymouth Press.

Nawratek, K. (2015). *Radical inclusivity: Architecture and urbanism*. dpr-barcelona.

Rancière, J. (2010). *Dissensus: On politics and aesthetics*. Continuum.

Schmitt, C. (2007). *The concept of the political*. University of Chicago Press.

Radical inclusivity

Focusing on the idea of 'inclusion', the political theorist Carl Schmitt defined the political as the motives and actions that result from our perceptions of who is a friend and who is an enemy. As he puts it, 'the specific political distinction to which political actions and motives can be reduced is that between friend and enemy' (Schmitt, 2007, p. 26). Indeed, the central argument of Schmitt's *The concept of the political* is encapsulated in this dichotomy between friend and enemy. However, this dichotomy is neither derived from nor linked to any other; instead, it is independent, and only corresponds to other dichotomies. The notion of inclusion can be rendered in philosopher Jacques Rancière's terms as the inside-out dichotomy. He uses the concept of *le partage du sensible* to describe the act of dividing between legitimate and illegitimate persons and forms of activity (Rancière, 2010, p. 60). In this sense, *radical inclusivity* assumes that the universe is infinite; it assumes progress and constant change – and also a change of hierarchies. There is a horizon of the whole, but there is no process of unification (Kozlowski et al., 2020). On the urban scale, the city is the best environment to test the notion of radical inclusivity, since its space is 'naturally' used by a diverse range of people.

Saskia de Wit
Delft University of Technology
Landscape architecture
S.I.deWit@tudelft.nl

Further readings

Stoetzer, B. (2018). Ruderal ecologies: Rethinking nature, migration and the urban landscape in Berlin. *Cultural Anthropology, 33*(2), 295–323.

Sukopp, H. (2008). On the early history of urban ecology in Europe. In J. Marzluff, E. Shulenberger, W. Endlicher, M. Alberti, G. Bradley, C. Ryan, C. ZumBrunnen, U. Simon (Eds.) (Eds), *Urban ecology: An international perspective on the interaction between humans and nature* (pp. 79–97). Springer.

Ruderal ecologies

The word 'ruderal' is derived from the Latin *rudus*, meaning rubble. A ruderal species is a plant species that is the first to colonise disturbed land, setting the stage for other ecosystems. These species are indicators of global connections, of a city coming back to life, and of global environmental change.
German ecologist Herbert Sukopp's (2008) and his colleagues' extensive mapping of the colonies of ruderal plants growing in the rubble of Berlin after the Second World War laid the foundations for contemporary research on ruderal vegetation. With their unwieldy presence, these plants challenged botanists to account for ruderal life in the city beyond the value regimes of urban nature and culture. Neither wild nor domesticated, ruderal species dwell alongside and in the cracks of urban infrastructures, including the categorical units of nature and culture through which we make sense of them. Their presence demands a broader conversation about the unexpected consequences of anthropogenic landscapes, capitalist trade and migration that shape urban environments.
According to cultural anthropologist Bettina Stoetzer (2018), the ruderal can be viewed as an analytical framework for rethinking the heterogeneity of contemporary urban life, to redirect attention towards human/non-human relations that emerge spontaneously in inhospitable environments. A ruderal analytic provides possibilities for an anthropological enquiry into urban environments and their ruins, an analysis that examines not only unruly non-human life, but also the broader unintended ecologies of human-built structures and the multispecies worlds of which they become part: an ecology of unexpected neighbours in the city. The ruderal perspective draws on ruins and infrastructure as conceptual devices to further undo the nature/culture divide. In contemporary European cities, this means looking at the ways in which the ruinous effects of capitalism, racism and nation-making become embodied in human-environment relations in often unpredictable ways.

Angelos Theocharis
University of Edinburgh
Cultural Studies
angelos.theocharis@ed.ac.uk

Further readings

Anemogiannis, D., & Theocharis, A. (forthcoming). 'Echoes of elves and demons in the riverbank': The exploration of history and folklore in Kythera through walking. In B. Piga, D. Siret & J.-P. Thibaud (Eds), *Experiential walks for urban design. Revealing, representing, and activating the sensory environment.* Springer.

Schafer, R. M. (1977). *The tuning of the world.* Knopf.

Schafer, R. M. (1994). *Soundscape: Our sonic environment and the tuning of the world.* Destiny Books.

Truax, B. (1984). *Acoustic communication.* Ablex.

Sensory community

Community, one of the fundamental concepts in sociology and anthropology, has been part of the discussion about the role that senses play in the experience and understanding of place from the very beginnings of sensory studies. The composers Schafer (1977, 1994) and Truax (1984) coined the notion of 'acoustic community', a symbolic entity created by and within an acoustic space, a soundscape. The sense of communality derives from the community's exposure to certain sounds – often everyday and common sounds, such as the church bell or the sound of trees in the neighbouring forest in windy weather – and is established through 'soundmarks' and 'sound barriers', which are perceived by community members but not necessarily by others (Truax, 1984, p. 59). Sounds are mediators, carriers of meaning, and through familiarity or distance they can act as the basis for the construction of difference.

If soundscapes can form acoustic communities, it is open to speculation whether other forms of sensorial input can in turn create communities based on the common experience of the sensory environment. Along with the landmarks and soundmarks that often dominate an environment and have an essential role in navigation through space, other sensory stimuli, separately or jointly with vision and sound, are also able to acquire a symbolic dimension for certain groups of people. The redolent lavender fields in Aix-en-Provence, France; the extensive olive groves on the island of Paxos in Greece, dominating the sensescape with their fragrant ambience; the distinctively steep streets of San Francisco, California; and many other examples from around the world foster communities around them through distinct sensory experiences. A *sensory community* usually follows either a centroperipheral model, with a particular stimulus constituting the centre, or a rhizomatic model in the case of multiple stimuli with no hierarchical order among the senses. In both models, the sensory experience is shared by a certain group of people, creating a sense of belonging and a common identity supported and reproduced through narratives and cultural memory.

Lamila Simisic Pasic
International University of Sarajevo
Philosophy & Architecture
lmsimisic@gmail.com

Further readings

Baudrillard, J. (1988). Simulacra and simulations. In *Selected writings* (pp. 166–184). Stanford University Press.

Deleuze, G. (1994). *Difference and repetition.* Columbia University Press.

Gabriel, M. (2015). *Why the world does not exist.* Polity Press.

Gibson, W. (1982). *Bruning Chrome.* Omni.

Simulacrum

The postmodern philosopher Jean Baudrillard introduced the concept simulacrum, which stands for something emptied of meaning, solely serving its own purposes. Architectural simulacra might be, for example, monuments, buildings without facilities, or mausoleums. Baudrillard relates this notion to the four phases of the image: first, the image is the reflection of a basic reality; second, it masks and perverts a basic reality; third, the image masks the absence of a basic reality; and finally, it bears no relation to any reality whatever. In the third and fourth phases, Baudrillard speaks of the simulacrum; in the fourth phase, the image is its own pure simulacrum (Baudrillard, 1988). In modern society, the simulacrum has overflowed the model and become an independent object. The philosopher Gilles Deleuze uses the term 'simulacrum' to describe something which is not a mere imitation but rather an 'act by which the very idea of a model or privileged position is challenged and overturned' (Deleuze, 1994, p. 69).
A contemporary example of a simulacrum is an avatar. To accommodate such new characters or actors in our wider understandings of the world, William Gibson coined the word 'cyberspace' (Gibson, 1982). The philosopher Markus Gabriel argues that the world is bigger than the object domain defined by natural science. The universe, according to Gabriel, comprises all intangible things, including dreams, possibilities and everything that occurs by us, not beside us (Gabriel, 2015). Today, the borders between the physical and the digital, the mystical and the real, are fading. This allows different realms to leak into one another, which may offer us more imaginative perspectives from which to address the human subject and the spaces we live in.

Klaske Havik
Delft University of Technology
Architecture
K.M.Havik@tudelft.nl

Willie Vogel
Delft University of Technology
Architecture
willie.c.vogel@gmail.com

Further readings

Haraway, D. (1988). Situated knowledges: The science question in feminism and the privilege of partial perspective. *Feminist Studies, 14*, 575–599.

Ingold, T. (2018). *Anthropology and/as Education*. Routledge.

Situated architecture

American feminist philosopher Donna Haraway introduced the term 'situated knowledge' to stress the importance of understanding the duality of objectivity and relativism (Haraway, 1988). For her, the 'objective view' is a view from above, which claims to be neutral. She argues that every viewpoint or way of looking is particular and situated. In her view, there is thus not one single Truth. The social anthropologist Tim Ingold also focuses on our situatedness which makes us see in one particular way. He argues that we need to be aware that our truths are constituted by ourselves. And due to the fact that we always change our viewpoint, our truths are always *in* transmission, not *of* a transmission. By our own movements and interactions everything we interpret is constantly in transmission. Therefore Ingold calls for *attention* rather than a fixed interpretation or explanation of the context (Ingold, 2018, p. 30).

If the concept of 'situated knowledge' is an attempt to do justice to the many different truths, *situated architecture* may then be an attempt to realise and actualise the social, ecological and political components of a specific location, recognising that architecture appears within specific contexts and circumstances. This suggests that our experience of architecture is bound to 'situations' that architecture both articulates and produces. Thinking of architecture as situated thus implies a responsibility towards the multiple voices of each situation. Therefore, any description of architecture must take into account its situatedness, so that it might be open to different perspectives, and so that the understanding of multiple voices and components can form the basis of 'situated' design proposals.

Marie Stender
Aalborg University
Anthropology and Architecture
mste@build.aau.dk

Further readings

Coyne, R. (1995). *Designing information technology in the postmodern age.* MIT Press.

Holbraad, M. (2011). *Can the thing speak?* Open Anthropology Cooperative Press.

Knappett, C. (2002). Photographs, skeuomorphs and marionettes: Some thoughts on mind, agency and object. *Journal of Material Culture*, 7(1), p. 97-117.

Stender, M. (2016) Menneskeskabte bjerge og markedskræfternes rasen: En etnografisk undersøgelse af arkitektur og stedskabelse i antropocæn tid. *Periskop.* 16, p. 72-90.

Skeuomorphism

The concept of *skeuomorphism* derives from the Greek words *skéuos*, meaning vessel or tool, and *morph*, meaning shape. It was introduced into archaeology to denote the manufacture of vessels in one, older material intended to evoke the appearance of vessels regularly made with another, more recent technology (Knappett, 2002). For example, we might find ceramic jars that imitate metal jars with rivets where the handle is fixed to the vessel. From being a functional necessity of the metal jar, the rivets become an ornament on the ceramic jar. Skeuomorphs are also commonly used in new digital technologies that mime analogue predecessors, for instance in digital books that one can flick through or in which one can write using a 'handwriting' font.

Skeuomorphism is well known in the world of architecture: the deep coffering of the concrete ceiling of the Pantheon reflects the earlier practice of supporting ceilings with timber beams (Coyne, 1995). How skeuomorphism appears in contemporary architecture and urban design is nevertheless relatively unexplored, although highly relevant. For instance, it appears in the so-called 8-house in Copenhagen, designed in 2010 by the Danish architecture studio BIG. The house was branded and shaped as 'a modern mountain village', although its mountainous volume did not derive from topography but from market forces and planning requirements (Stender, 2016). Here, the concept of skeuomorphism is not about artefacts miming prior materials, but about how in developing the new we incorporate elements of the old, and how places – like materials – analyse each other by translating prior forms into novel contents (Holbraad, 2011). When writing about the city, we need accurate tools and concepts to grasp how temporality and longing are deployed in urban spaces, materialities and narratives. Here the concept of skeuomorphism can address how places come to be related to other places in time and space.

Sonja Novak
Josip Juraj Strossmayer University of Osijek
Humanities
snovak@ffos.hr

Further readings

Durrell, M. (2004). Sociolect. In U. Ammon Ulrich Ammon, Norbert Dittmar, Klaus J. Mattheier, Peter Trudgill, (Eds), *Sociolinguistics: An international handbook of the science of language and society* (pp. 200–205). Walter de Gruyter.

Petrović, V. (1994). Die essekerische Mundart. In K. Wild (Ed.), *Begegnung in Pécs/Fünfkirchen: Die Sprache der deutschsprachigen Minderheiten in Europa* (pp. 19–32). Janus-Pannonius-Universität.

Petrović, V. (2008). *Esekerski rječnik/Essekerisches Wörterbuch*. F. F. Press.

Šojat, I. (2009). *Unterstadt*. Fraktura.

Sociolect

A *sociolect* is a form of non-standard language used by a specific social group (a socio-economic class, a profession, or a group living in a certain geographical space). Sociolects can thus be understood as particular communicative practices associated with specific local communities. As such they can be acquired both passively and actively (Durrell, 2004), and they demonstrate identification with particular groups. The sociolect is specific in terms of its orthography, lexis, phonetics and grammar. In the context of urban narratives, the (conscious) usage of sociolects plays an important role in determining the sociopolitical dimensions and cultural embeddedness of a narrative's authorial and other voices, and the names and concepts in the story. The Esseker language is an example of a sociolect – a city-specific speech that appeared as a mixture of German, Croatian, Yiddish, Turkish and Hungarian. It was the result of a heterogeneous multinational and multi-ethnic society living in the city Osijek (eastern Croatia) from the 17th century onwards. This language was used by craftsmen, merchants and peasant families living on the outskirts of the city, and it was only recorded in Osijek as a specific means of oral communication among its citizens up until the second half of the 20th century. One example of the usage of Esseker can be found in the prize-winning novel *Unterstadt* by the contemporary Croatian writer Ivana Šojat. She uses this sociolect, for example, to position the narrative in terms of place (the city of Osijek and its Lower Town), and to emphasise the time leaps in the plot (from the second half of the 19th century and first half of the 20th century to the present day).

Maria Gil Ulldemolins
Hasselt University
Faculty of Architecture & Arts
maria.gilulldemolins@uhasselt.be

Further readings

Hlibchuk, G. (2011). Delirious cities: Lisa Robertson's occasional work and seven walks from the office for soft architecture. *Studies in Canadian Literature/Études en littérature canadienne, 36*(1). https://journals.lib.unb.ca/index.php/SCL/article/view/18637

Robertson, L. (2010). *Occasional work and seven walks from the office for soft architecture.* Coach House Books.

Soft architecture

The term *soft architecture* was coined by poet Lisa Robertson (born Toronto, 1961). It consists of the remembrance and research of a city's surfaces (in Robertson's case, Vancouver) after its spaces have disappeared through time and gentrification.
Soft architecture is first and foremost a manifesto (Robertson, 2010, pp. 18–21). It reads as an intimate defence of different ideas of softness (malleability, biology, memory, clothes, transience, adaptability). It insists on their survival and persistence, on how time has a way of evidencing the softness of what we once thought firm: it is all a 'myth', a 'slow-motion mystic takeover'.
Consequently, soft architecture proposes new ways of describing 'the warp' of past events, declaring that the manifestation of present particularities and dialects constitutes a 'utopian act'.
As a manifesto, it also has a critique woven into its message. For instance, it compares the shifting undulations, construction and destruction of tented camps to the precarity of contemporary labour. And, perhaps more directly, it declares a will to 'reverse the wrongheaded story of structural deepness. That institution is all doors but no entrances' (Robertson, 2010, p. 21).
Robertson's concept, as evidenced by her interest in history and narrative, is also linguistic. Soft architecture makes the structure of language tangible. Language, and the relationships it creates, makes up bodies and emotions, and vice versa. The 'lyrical tone' of soft furnishings can confess the pulse of shared emotions.
Ultimately, soft architecture is very much embodied. This notion folds into itself the author's desires and experiences, which leads to multiplicity, to the poet becoming the city, its inhabitants, its surfaces, its descriptions, its affects. She argues that it is *living*, and not disembodied, intellectual knowledge that is the object of thought, suggesting the necessary incarnation of softness: 'our bodies produce spaces' (Robertson, 2010, p. 20).

Adriana Martins
Universidade Católica Portuguesa
Culture Studies
adrimartins@fch.lisboa.ucp.pt

Further readings

Augé, M. (1995). *Non-places: Introduction to an anthropology of supermodernity.* Verso.

Avramidis, K., & Tsilimpunidi, M. (Eds). (2017). *Graffiti and street art: Reading, writing and representing the city.* Routledge.

Waclawek, A. (2011). *Graffiti and street art.* Thames & Hudson.

Young, A. (2016). *Street art world.* Reaktion Books.

Street art

Urban spaces have always been a mirror of how societies imagine and organise themselves. Therefore, it is worth paying attention to 'city writing' as it embodies literary and visual mediations of the city. 'City writing' has been an important source to help us understand the symbolic and metaphorical design of urban geographies of equity, equality, inequality, conflict and hope. Within the framework of urban visual writing, *street art* acquires special importance, as it transforms cityscapes into physical and metaphorical arenas in which the uneven development of societies has been written in symbolic terms.

According to art historian Anna Waclawek (2011), street art emerges in the 21st century as a relevant art movement that approaches and (re)writes the city from an alternative perspective. Taking into account its narrative dimension, she suggests that authorised and mainly unauthorised street art projects question the very notion of public space. By disrupting the public sphere and investing it with new subjectivities, street art constitutes a way of resisting sanctioned imagery (Waclawek, 2011, p. 3) and creating alternative forms of culture (Waclawek, 2011, p. 74). In addition to its transgressive and subversive character, street art assumes a performative dimension that transforms urban non-places (Augé, 1995) into anthropological places invested with new meanings that promote communication and conviviality.

Luisa Metelo Seixas
NOVA School of Social Sciences and Humanities, Institute of Contemporary History
luisaseixasihc@fcsh.unl.pt

Further readings

Caswell, M. (2014). Seeing yourself in history: Community archives and the fight against symbolic annihilation. *Public Historian, 36*(4), 26–37. https://doi.org/10.1525/tph.2014.36.4.26

Caswell, M., Migoni, A. A., Geraci, N., & Cifor, M. (2016) 'To be able to imagine otherwise': Community archives and the importance of representation. *Archives and Records, 38*(1), 5–26. https://doi.org/10.1080/23257962.2016.1260445

Gerbner, G. (1972). Violence in television drama: Trends and symbolic functions. In G. A. Comstock and E. Rubinstein (Eds), *Television and social behavior, volume I: Content and control* (pp. 28–187). US Government Printing Office.

Tuchman, G. (1978). The symbolic annihilation of women by the mass media. In G. Tuchman, A. K. Daniels & J. Benet (Eds), *Hearth and home: Images of women in the mass media* (pp. 3–38). Oxford University Press.

Symbolic annihilation

Largely applied to the mass media (and first coined by media sociologist George Gerbner in 1972), the term *symbolic annihilation* refers to the absence, under-representation or misrepresentation of some communities and social groups in media culture, and the impacts of this on individual and collective identity and behaviour. In 1978, the sociologist Gaye Tuchman referred to the symbolic annihilation of women in mass media and the ways in which this impacted on the shaping of young women and girls and created gender roles and stereotypes in collective consciousness. More recently, archive scholar Michelle Caswell (2014) has referred to the symbolic annihilation of some communities and social groups in the United States' institutional archives, and the impacts of this on historical narratives, consciousness and embodiment, with repercussions for individual and collective identity and belonging. Similarly, the term might be applied to the urban context, considering how cities and their symbolic frameworks – from toponymy to monuments – often marginalise specific communities who have taken part in the city's historical processes of development but find little or no place in its public narratives, since the urban built environment and heritage preservation policies may also shape public memory and the narratives related to the urban landscape.

Matej Nikšič
Urban Planning Institute of the Republic of Slovenia
Architecture and Urbanism
mtej.niksic@uirs.si

Further readings

Bentley, I., Alcock, A., Murrain, P., McGlynn, S., & Smith, G. (1987). *Responsive environments: A manual for designers*. Architectural Press

Fontana, M. P., Mayorga, M., & Roa, M. (2016). Le Corbusier: Urban visions through thresholds. *Journal of Architecture and Urbanism, 40*(2), 87–98. https://doi.org/10.3846/20297955.2016.1196541

Threshold

A *threshold* is an element or space that defines the limit between the inside and the outside, between the (semi-)private and the (semi-)public. The threshold addresses relations of separation and union between an enclosed interior space and an open urban space. In physical terms, it most often appears as a gap in the built boundary of the open public space, and it can manifest itself in different forms, such as a doorstep, a window or a balcony. As a transitory element between private and public space, the threshold is the often the stage for practices of the personalisation and appropriation of urban space. We can read the city through the ways in which thresholds are personalised, which helps us to better understand the city's social dimension. In terms of urban design, a considerable effort is necessary (Bentley et al., 1987) to allow thresholds to become personalised: the general urban design layout must be conceived so that it encourages and gives an opportunity for thresholds to reflect the social fabric of the city. Allowing personalisation is especially important in highly dense built environments, such as large housing estates where standardised housing gives the impression of monotony and soullessness. According to architecture scholars Fontana, Mayorga and Roa (2016), the threshold defines, qualifies and characterises the minimum condition of urbanity of any work of architecture, irrespective of its use or scale.

Inesa Alistratovaitė-Kurtinaitienė
Vilnius Gediminas Technical University
Urban design
inesa.alistratovaite@vgtu.lt

Further readings

Cowan, R. (2005). *The dictionary of urbanism*. Streetwise Press.

Daunora, Z. J., Vyšniūnas, A., & Kirvaitienė, S. (2004). *Vilniaus miesto vizualinio identiteto apsauga ir plėtros principai* [Preservation of the visual identity of Vilnius city and principles of its development]. Technika.

Goodall, B. (1987). *Dictionary of human geography*. Penguin.

Whistler, W., & Reed, D. (1994). Townscape as a philosophy of urban design. *Urban Design Quarterly*, 52: 15–30.

Townscape

Architect Gordon Cullen (in his best-known book, *Townscape*) presented *townscape* as a method of urban visual analysis and design based on the psychology of perception. The townscape in this sense is usually perceived through the silhouette and the panorama. However, in research work by Lithuanian architects and urbanists, the townscape is treated as a structural part of the town, characterised by unity in its spatial and planned structure, the height of its buildings and its architectural image (Daunora et al., 2004). This single townscape represents the physical fabric of the town, creating an individual image of the area. In large cities there are multiple townscapes, which often become more complex than in smaller towns.

Traditionally, in dictionaries of geography, 'townscape' is the urban equivalent of 'landscape' – the visual patterning of a town or city (as a physical entity integrating a street plan or layout, an architectural style or building fabric, and land use and function) and can be related to the urban dweller's 'image of the city' (Goodall, 1987, pp. 223, 475). In *The dictionary of urbanism*, the concept of 'townscape' is understood in three ways (Cowan, 2005, p. 400):

- An urban form and its visual appearance: the appearance of streets, including how the components of a street combine in a way that is distinctive of a particular locality.
- An approach to urban design that focuses on this. Whistler and Reed (1994) note that the *Oxford English Dictionary* cites 1880 for the first use of the word 'townscape', and 1889 for its specific use in this sense.
- Part of a town that can be seen in a single view.

In all three of these definitions, a townscape can be perceived from inside or outside. However, these definitions are not identical to the conception of the Lithuanian morphological school, which defines the townscape as a unique structural part of a town that creates the town's identity. Architects and urban designers can express the identity of a townscape graphically, but a townscape can also be conveyed through writing or telling stories.

Maria Finn
Visual Artist
monamariafinn@gmail.com

Further readings

Bauman, Z. (1989). *Modernity and the holocaust*. Polity.

Braidotti, R. (2011). *Nomadic subjects*. Columbia University Press.

Clément, G. (2015). *The planetary garden and other writings*. University of Pennsylvania Press.

Undefined terrain

Within the city there exist overlooked areas that offer different sensations from formal parks: spaces in between roads and railways, or abandoned plots of land, where another kind of vegetation flourishes. This kind of unruly vegetation represents an *undefined terrain* that does not care about following rules, and which effortlessly presents a messy beauty. Lately this has also been found in newly established green urban areas, often referred to as 'urban nature'. Another example can be found in parks where grass is left to grow for the benefit of insects, and where the park's orderly appearance changes significantly. These examples of undefined terrain can open up ideas about the role of the gardener in the city, and about how to balance the wild and the planned. Sociologist Zygmunt Bauman referred to modernity as a garden culture where the weeds had to be cleared away, along with everything else that did not fit a certain order (Bauman, 1989). The French thinker and gardener Gilles Clément (2015, p. 79) refers to the 'planetary garden' where everything is connected: 'A garden is always a planetary index. Ecology destroys the notion of the "enclosed" garden'. Thus, careless nature in the city represents a motion towards a less fixed conception, something feminist philosopher Rosi Braidotti elaborates on in *Nomadic Subjects* (2011), where she suggests that we need to adopt more fluid positions – instead of sticking to preformed opinions, we need to learn to move between concepts. Undefined terrain changes our expectations of green spaces within the city, and proposes inclusion as well as transformation.

Marie Stender
Aalborg University
Anthropology and Architecture
mste@build.aau.dk

Further readings

Latour, B. (2009). Spheres and networks: Two ways to reinterpret globalization. *Harvard Design Magazine, 30*, pp. 38-144.

Tsing, A. (2014). More-than-human-sociality: A call for critical description. In K. Hastrup (Ed.), *Anthropology and nature*, pp. 27-42. Routledge.

Yaneva, A. (2012). *Mapping controversies in architecture*. Ashgate.

Unintended design

The concept of *unintended design* can help us to focus on aspects of urban environments that are created and shaped by human beings, although not intentionally. Further, the concept directs our attention to how urban environments are also home to and co-created by other, non-human species and phenomena. The oxymoron 'unintended design' was first coined by anthropologist Anna Tsing in connection with her studies of how different species – mushrooms and people –create worlds for themselves and each other in the Japanese forest: 'One might call the relations that grow up together in the Satoyama Forest a kind of multispecies design, but an unintended design' (Tsing, 2014, p. 36), she writes.

Texts about architecture and design often tend to present urban environments as purposefully designed by architects and urban planners. In the era of the Anthropocene, however, such phenomena as human-made climate change and the bankruptcies of American investment banks also take part in shaping our built environments. Philosopher Bruno Latour argues that the present ecological crisis demonstrates that the Earth is now finally round: of course we knew that before, but today it takes on a new meaning, because the consequences of our actions – our refuse, our toxic wastes and toxic loans – travel around the blue planet and come back to haunt us (Latour, 2009). We are responsible for both loans and refuse, yet they shape the world in ways that now seem beyond control.

The concept of unintended design helps us to realise that such phenomena are to be regarded not as outside architecture and urban design, but rather as part and parcel of the social and material realities that architects and urban planners orchestrate. Architecture – or the architectural – in architectural theorist Albena Yaneva's words is not an object in itself, but rather 'a type of connector', a manner of doing, of dealing with and connecting various actors (Yaneva, 2012). By studying unintended design we can focus on the plethora of ways that we create worlds for ourselves and each other in the urban environments of the Anthropocene. It is time for new narratives that include both human and non-human inhabitants and their connections, to stimulate the design of environments for life in the Anthropocene.

Juan A. García-Esparza
Universitat Jaume I
Architectural conservation
juan.garcia@uji.es

Further readings

Altaba, P., & García-Esparza, J.A. (2018). The heritagization of a Mediterranean Vernacular Mountain Landscape: Concepts, Problems and Processes. *Heritage & Society* 11 (3), 189-210.

García-Esparza, J. A. (2018). Clarifying dynamic authenticity in cultural heritage: A look at vernacular built environments. In: C. Holtorf, L. Kealy & T. Kono (Eds.), *ICOMOS, volume 1: ICOMOS university forum workshop on authenticity and reconstructions.* http://openarchive.icomos.org/1909/

Rapoport, A. (2006). Vernacular design as a model system. In L. Asquith & M. Vellinga (Eds), *Vernacular architecture in the twenty-first century* (pp. 179–199). Taylor & Francis.

Urban habitat

Architect Amos Rapoport has talked about studying systems of activities – or habitats – instead of buildings or settings. This leads to a specific view of environments as restricted only by evolution, as suggested by sociology, behavioural ecology and evolutionary psychology.

Urban environments need to be approached as habitats rather than settings: as places that show significant material evidence of historical – and contemporary – evolution, dynamic cognition, time and a sense of otherness. This can be done on the understanding that both ways of life and material evidence evolve, in a continuous creation, reinterpretation and eventual negotiation of contemporary human/non-human interactions.

Habitats simulate a theory that adapts and transforms itself into everyday life activities that carry feelings and emotions. In habitats, artefacts can help to establish dialectical environments where the past never settles but opens up to a plural future. Understanding the urban environment as a habitat renders inclusive the emotional and humane aspects of a city. The historic city rarely adapts to the social and cultural diversity of the place, which in turn can impair the weak and marginalised.

It is also likely that the inclusive outcome enforces fluid and permeable social constructions, reconstructions or deconstructions – all processes that may legitimate constructive practices that constitute the future-making of the habitat.

Angeliki Sioli
Delft University of Technology
Architecture
A.Sioli@tudelft.nl

Further readings

Horwitz, J., & Singley, P. (2004). *Eating architecture*. MIT Press.

Martin-McAuliffe, L. S. (2016). *Food and architecture: At the table*. Bloomsbury.

Steel, C. (2013). *Hungry city: How food shapes our lives*. Vintage.

Urban eating

The *Merriam-Webster* dictionary definition of the verb 'to eat' refers to the activity of 'taking in through the mouth as food: ingest, chew, and swallow in turn'. *Urban eating* expands this definition, positioning the activity in the public sphere of the city. Placed outside a private or commercial environment (e.g. a bricks-and-mortar restaurant, bar or cafe), eating in the city takes new forms. We eat walking down a pavement, using a pedestrian crossing, lingering idly in front of a shop window, sitting on a bench in a public square or on the edge of a fountain, lying down in a park.

As consumer culture takes advantage of the basic biological impulse of hunger, urban eating and the abundance of street food have a notable effect on a city. Places such as street cantinas, food stalls, snack vans and pop-ups enliven the urban environment. Words connected to street food enrich local languages and break down geographical boundaries. Turkish doner, Greek gyros, Middle Eastern kebabs, French *frites*, Mexican tacos, takeaway Japanese sushi, and Italian espresso or cappuccino belong to 21st-century Europe's international vocabulary of urban eating, infiltrating different cultures.

Nonetheless, place-specific eating customs give unique nuances to the activity of urban eating in each given environment. The popularity of specific street foods, the times of day when urban eating customarily takes place, the season of the year when specific street foods are enjoyed, the quantity of the food usually consumed, and the slight alteration of universal recipes with local ingredients to please local palates are some of the most prominent elements defining regional cultures of urban eating. Adding to these nuances are the narratives, stories or myths associated with food in each given culture: urban eating may vary distinctively, even among cities in the same country. These particularities reveal habits and norms that reach far beyond the fulfilment of a basic biological need. Such specificities of urban eating point to people's expectations regarding the use and appropriation of public space, and to people's mindsets regarding their right to public space and how that right should be exercised. Local cultures of urban eating provide a rich and precise understanding of place, and can lead to unique and original urban design strategies of value for architects, engineers and planners.

Klaske Havik
Delft University of Technology
Architecture
K.M.Havik@tudelft.nl

Further readings

Havik, K. (2006). Lived experience, places read: Toward an urban literacy. In Grafe, C., Maaskant, M. and Havik, K., (Eds.), *OASE 70: Architecture & literature, reflections/ imaginations* (pp. 37–49). NAi Publishers.

Havik, K. (2014). *Urban literacy: Reading and writing architecture.* NAi Publishers.

Landry, C. (2000). *The creative city: A toolkit for urban innovators.* Earthskin/ Comedia.

Urban literacy

The term *urban literacy* was coined by Charles Landry, a theorist of urban innovation, in his book *The creative city* (2000). According to Landry, urban analysis and design are complex activities involving several different disciplines, which should help us to experience, understand and respond to the city. This requires a broader set of instruments, beyond urban planning and architecture. Landry defines urban literacy as the skill to look at the city from different perspectives: 'Urban literacy is the ability and skill to "read" the city and understand how cities work' (Landry, 2000, pp. 246–247). In *Urban literacy* (Havik, 2014), this idea of urban literacy is further explored by examining how insights from literature might provide fruitful approaches to the understanding of place. In this book, description, transcription and prescription are introduced as three research perspectives concerning the experiential, social and imaginative qualities of architecture respectively. In relation to research on urban places, description addresses the fundamental aspect of lived experience by means of close observation of site-specific characteristics. Here, phenomenological enquiries through evocative descriptions are at stake. Transcription focuses on social spatial practices, and brings in narrative as an investigative method, which allows the inclusion of perspectives from different local protagonists. The third concept, prescription, deals with the balance between reality and imagination. Here, critical imaginings of alternative situations are used as a perspective to address the design of urban places.

Angeliki Sioli
Delft University of Technology
Architecture
A.Sioli@tudelft.nl

Further readings

de Certeau, M. (1984). Walking in the city. In *The practice of everyday life* (pp. 91–110). University of California Press.

Shepard, L. (1973). *The history of street literature: The story of broadside ballads, chapbooks, proclamations, news-sheets, election bills, tracts, pamphlets, cocks, catchpennies, and other ephemera.* Singing Tree Press.

Urban texts

Reading is an integral activity for engaging with the environment of a city. Whether for practical reasons (e.g. orientation, navigation, information or commerce) or for pleasure and leisure, on a daily basis our eyes meet an overwhelming number of words and texts in the urban public sphere. Street names, location and direction signs, commercial labels, information panels, announcement boards, commemorative plaques, transport schedules, newspapers and urban rags, graffiti art, political and promotional flyers, advertisements for different purposes and on different scales, and paperbacks on public transport are common occurrences in our everyday interactions with a city. To this urban palimpsest, the 21st century has added the words on our mobile devices. We read on our screens while walking along the street, resting on a bench, taking the tram, or engaging in physical activities which do not necessarily encourage reading, such as riding a bike or driving a car. Messages, tweets, posts, newsfeeds and navigation instructions add a prevalent digital layer to our everyday *urban texts*. Both printed and digital urban texts, although visible in the city, can also act on an invisible level for a city dweller. As philosopher Michel de Certeau observes, some of these words and their meanings (or symbolic dimensions) insinuate other routes into the functionalistic and historical order of a city. They articulate a second, poetic geography on top of the geography of literal meaning, and thus influence us consciously or unconsciously (de Certeau, 1984). Urban texts penetrate our thoughts, trigger our imaginations, inspire impromptu decisions and define actions. Although usually silent, they have a loud impact on our appropriation of, experience of and emotional connection with a city.

Lieven Ameel
Tampere University
Comparative Literature
lieven.ameel@tuni.fi

Further readings

Ameel, L. (2016). Narrative mapping and polyphony in urban planning. *Yhdyskuntasuunnittelu/Finnish Journal for Urban Studies, 2*, 20–40.

Brunskill, R. W. (2000). Illustrated handbook of vernacular architecture (4th ed.). Faber & Faber.

Spivak, G. (1988). Can the subaltern speak? Macmillan.

Vernacular

In the context of planning and urban studies, the use of the concept *vernacular* takes its cue from the idea that the built environment communicates in a way that resembles language.
'Vernacular' refers to the local or indigenous language of a country or district. It denotes a highly site-specific utterance. It suggests a natural, organically formed form of language, and it focuses on spoken rather than written language. This idea of the vernacular, as opposed to standardised language, is rooted in postcolonial thinking about local communities talking back by drawing on their own site- and culture-specific linguistic properties.
In architecture theory, 'vernacular' has tended to focus on specific local building types, but the term also opens up possibilities for a mode of designing that is conscious about localised narrative form. To think about interventions in the built environment in terms of the vernacular would be to think about a mode of storytelling in planning that aims to integrate and start out from the specificities of the local built environment (architectural motifs, building materials, building patterns, street patterns etc.) as well as the storytelling structures of local communities. In this sense, the vernacular is also connected to the idea of polyphony in planning.
The concept also raises questions of legitimacy: who can, or is allowed to, speak in the vernacular? What happens when the vernacular becomes part of established language? Such questions have been most vividly addressed in postcolonial theory, but the consequences of such discussions have yet to find their way into planning and architecture theories about the vernacular.

Bie Plevoets
Hasselt University
Faculty of Architecture & Arts
bie.plevoets@uhasselt.be

Further readings

Hou, J. (2010). *Insurgent public space: Guerrilla urbanism and the remaking of contemporary cities.* Routledge.

Mould, O. (2014). Tactical urbanism: The new vernacular of the creative city. *Geography Compass, 8*(8), 529–539. Plevoets, B., & Sowinska-Heim,

Plevoets, B., & Sowinska-Heim, J. (2018). Community initiatives as a catalyst for regeneration of heritage sites: Vernacular transformation and its influence on the formal adaptive reuse practice. Cities, 78 (august 2018), 128-139.

Rudofsky, B. (1987). *Architecture without architects: A short introduction to non-pedigreed architecture.* University of New Mexico Press.

Scott, F. (2008). *On altering architecture.* Routledge.

Vernacular intervention

'Vernacular' is a term traditionally applied in the contexts of both language and architecture, and it refers to what belongs to and is created by the common people as opposed to the elite – the informal as opposed to the formal. Vernacular architecture is usually understood as an expression of local craft skills, created without the supervision of professional architects. Interest in the vernacular way of building arose in the 1960s as a reaction against the 'universality' of modernism, in which the vernacular was seen as the very opposite of modernity.

However, the notion of the vernacular as the informal or non-professional approach to the built environment may also be applied in the context of contemporary 'modern' cities, and more specifically in the context of building adaptation. The term *vernacular intervention* can be used to point to the informal use and adaptation of spaces by individuals, collectives or local communities. Vernacular interventions are mostly community-driven, low-budget, temporary and experimental. The materials used are often reclaimed from other building sites. Other terms that refer to this type of informal, community-driven activity are 'do-it-yourself (or DIY) urbanism', 'tactical urbanism', 'pop-up', 'urban pioneer movements', and 'guerrilla' or 'insurgent urbanism'.

Such (temporary) informal interventions may have a more sustainable impact, as they can raise awareness about certain needs, or show the potential of previously neglected or rundown areas. In some cases, vernacular interventions may lead to the gentrification of a site or area, and often the individuals or groups which started the process are later pushed out because of rising property prices: they become the victims of their own success. In other cases, the vernacular intervention is a conscious strategy to upgrade a site or area. In such circumstances, the boundaries between the vernacular and the formal become blurred, and the vernacular becomes part of the established architectural language and discourse.

Dalia Dijokienė
Vilnius Gediminas Technical University
Urban Design
dalia.dijokiene@vgtu.lt

Further readings

Cowan, R. (2005). *The dictionary of urbanism*. Streetwise Press.

Cullen, G. (1961). *Townscape*. Van Nostrand Reinhold.

Cuthbert, A. R. (2011). *Understanding cities: Method in urban design*. Routledge.

Jurkštas, V. (1977). Vilniaus senamiesčio tūrinė-erdvinė kompozicija [Volume-spatial composition of Vilnius Old Town]. *Architektūros paminklai*, 4, 36–60.

Jurkštas, V. (1994). *Senamiesčių regeneracija: Architektūros harmonizavimo problema* [Historical regeneration: The problem of architectural harmonisation]. Technika.

Visual frames

In the 1970s, Lithuanian architecture researcher Vytautas Jurkštas studied the spatial composition of Lithuania's old towns, focusing on urban spaces. According to Jurkštas, urban spaces can be characterised by the frequency, mode and content of the visible images – or *visual frames* (*vizualinis kadras*, in the sense of the 'frames' of a film) – that one perceives while walking down the street. For example, according to his research, one's street-view image of Vilnius Old Town changes every 75 seconds on average. The more frequently the visual frame changes in pedestrians' perception, he argues, the more diverse and attractive the space is (Jurkštas, 1977, pp. 51-52).

Jurkštas proposes two ways of analysing the composition of urban spaces: studying how specific spaces are composed by looking at them from certain observation points; or studying the sum of the impressions, in time and space, which are then combined into a unified composition (Jurkštas, 1994, p. 35). The second mode of analysis is relevant not only for researchers but also for residents and guests in a town, as it helps to create their mental picture of urban spaces.

This concept of visual frames is similar to architect and illustrator Gordon Cullen's concept of 'serial vision', which he coined in his critique of modernism in the 1960s and 1970s (Cullen, 1961; Cuthbert, 2011, p. 208). Cullen's technique was devised as a way of visualising the perception of existing (or proposed) urban spaces. Serial vision is expressed through a series of drawings showing what a person would see at a succession of viewpoints while walking through an area (Cowan, 2005, p. 347). The concepts of serial vision and visual frames, as proposed by Cullen and Jurkštas respectively, can be revived today, and can help town dwellers to rediscover their urban environment's distinctive features, nurture those features, and identify with the living environment. The same urban fabric can be perceived differently by different people. Urban narratives can multiply the ways in which people perceive an urban space and help them to explore the city through multiple lenses, including individual ways of experiencing visual frames.

Ann Petermans
Hasselt University
Faculty of Architecture & Arts
ann.petermans@uhasselt.be

Further readings

Lyubomirsky, S., Sheldon, K. M., & Schkade, D. (2005). Pursuing happiness: The architecture of sustainable change. *Review of General Psychology, 9,* 111–131.

Petermans, A., & Cain, R. (Eds). (2019). *Design for wellbeing: An applied approach.* Routledge, London

United Nations General Assembly. (2013). *Happiness: Towards a holistic approach to development.* http://www.un.org/ga/search/view:doc.asp?symbol=A/67/697

Well-being

'Being well' and 'feeling well' is a major goal for most, if not all, human beings. The concept of *well-being* has received attention in a diverse range of disciplines (philosophy, psychology etc.) while being used interchangeably in a lot of academic research and more popular publications with the concept of 'happiness'. Since 2013, attention to well-being from design has grown steadily, nourished by the growing number of institutions, governments and organisations worldwide that pay attention to this topic. To date, there is no consensus on an exact definition of well-being. Researchers, however, do agree first that well-being/happiness is determined in large part by genetics, life circumstances and intentional activities, and second that well-being/happiness has an objective and a subjective component. When we are exploring the narratives that people develop in particular places, focusing on their well-being/happiness can teach us much about what kinds of interventions trigger particular activities, which in turn can contribute to people's happiness.

Heidi Svenningsen Kajita
University of Copenhagen
Landscape Architecture and Planning
hsk@ign.ku.dk

Further readings

Braidotti, R. (2011). *Nomadic subjects: Embodiment and sexual difference in contemporary feminist theory* (2nd ed.). Columbia University Press.

Hustvedt, S. (2006). *A plea for Eros.* Sceptre.

Kajita, H. S. (forthcoming 2020). Yonder product and practice. In M. Glendinning & S. Riesto (Eds), *Mass housing of the Scandinavian welfare states: Exploring histories and design approaches.* Docomomo/University of Edinburgh.

Yonder

'My father once asked me if I knew where Yonder was. I said I thought yonder was another word for there. He smiled and said: "No, yonder is between here and there"' (Hustvedt, 2006, p. 1). *Yonder* is a shifter: the term moves ambiguously with the speaker, and as novelist Siri Hustvedt tells us, you can never find yourself yonder.

Now, let us borrow this unsettling notion of yonder place from Hustvedt's fictitious works, to ponder architectural products and practices in a paradigm of transformation. In this context, the adverb 'yonder' may trigger new writing practices, embracing future-making as a concern with repair rather than novelty. Guided by present normative professional frameworks, architects and planners *pre*scribe work step by step for the production of tangible objects. Their instructions for the work – masterplans, performance specifications, local plans etc. – are written and drawn in order to limit liability, ensure agile collaboration processes, guarantee the quality of materials etc. Use is predicted beforehand, and manuals describe the objects 'in use' afterwards. A park is prescribed for running, sunbathing and bird-feeding. A window is specified for ease of cleaning. But how might this linear grasp, which underpins instructions of architecture and planning, embed the possibilities presented by different memories, narratives and imaginaries?

The promise of yonder directs our attention to expanded and extended time frames, as well as to shifting subject positions – say, to housing that has been, is and will be inhabited and looked after over time by various people. Here, yonder products and practices function like open-ended images: they both delimit certain immediate tasks necessary for construction and muse on the uncertain particularities of, say, inhabitation and continued maintenance. From here, architectural prescriptions may set off many different motions – not just those that are translated into built objects.

Colophon

Authors
Inesa Alistratovaitė-Kurtinaitienė
Lieven Ameel
Jana Čulek
Nevena Daković
Dalia Dijokienė
Mirza Emirhafizović
Maria Finn
Lars Frers
Juan A. García-Esparza
Maria Gil Ulldemolins
Heidi Kajita
Katarzyna Kopecka-Piech
Karen Lens
Anne Margrethe Wagner
Adriana Martins
Asma Mehan
Luisa Metelo Seixas
Dalia Milián Bernal
Matej Nikšič
Sonja Novak
Ann Petermans
Marcel Pikhart
Bie Plevoets
Ida Sandström
Sara Santos Cruz
Lamila Simisic Pasic
Angeliki Sioli
Matthew Skjonsberg
Eliana Sousa Santos
Marie Stender
Ruth Stevens
Angelos Theocharis
Sylvie Tram Nguyen
Jan Vanrie
Kristin Veel
Willie Vogel
Saskia de Wit
Kęstutis Zaleckis

Editors / Authors
Klaske Havik
Kris Pint
Svava Riesto
Henriette Steiner

Editoral assistant
Willie Vogel

English proofreading
Merl Storr

Graphic design
www.studiosannedijkstra.nl

Publisher
nai010 Publishers, Rotterdam

Acknowledgement
This publication is based upon work from COST Action CA18126 Writing Urban Places, supported by COST (European Cooperation in Science and Technology).
COST (European Cooperation in Science and Technology) is a funding agency for research and innovation networks. Our Actions help connect research initiatives across Europe and enable scientists to grow their ideas by sharing them with their peers. This boosts their research, career and innovation.

COST Action Writing Urban Places core team
Klaske Havik
Kinga Kimic
Jorge Mejía Hernández
Lorin Niculae
Susana Oliveira
Marcel Pikhart
Mark Proosten
Svava Riesto
Luis Santiago Baptista
Henriette Steiner
Slobodan Velevski

Weblink
www.cost.eu
www.writingurbanplaces.eu

isbn 9789462085763

This publication is supported by:

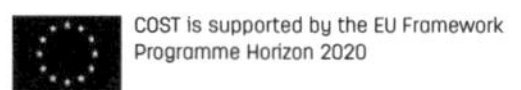

COST Action CA18126 Writing Urban Places: New Narratives of the European city

Writing Urban Places proposes an innovative investigation and implementation of a process for developing human understanding of communities, their society, and their situatedness. By recognising the value of local urban narratives – stories rich in information regarding citizens socio-spatial practices, perceptions and expectations – the Action aims to articulate a set of concrete literary devices within a host of spatial disciplines; bringing together scientific research in the fields of literary studies, urban planning and architecture; and positioning this knowledge vis-à-vis progressive redevelopment policies carried out in medium-sized cities in Europe. **Working Group 2** of the Action, led by Svava Riesto and Henriette Steiner, is concerned with how theoretical reflections can stimulate the thinking and praxis of narrating urban places of medium-sized European cities. In 2019-2020, the group focused on the collaborative project of compiling definitions of Minor Concepts for Writing Urban Places into this Vademecum, a short guide that can be kept at hand for consultation when being in or writing about urban places.

writinG urban places